Stupid American History

Stupid American History

Tales of Stupidity, Strangeness, and Mythconceptions

★ ★ ★

LELAND GREGORY

**Andrews McMeel
Publishing, LLC**
Kansas City

Stupid American History
Copyright © 2009 by Leland Gregory. All rights reserved. Printed
in the United States of America. No part of this book may be
used or reproduced in any manner whatsoever without written
permission except in the case of reprints in the context of reviews.
For information, write Andrews McMeel Publishing, LLC,
an Andrews McMeel Universal company, 1130 Walnut Street,
Kansas City, Missouri 64106.

ISBN-13: 978-0-7407-7991-6
ISBN-10: 0-7407-7991-5

Library of Congress Control Number: 2008936163

09 10 11 12 13 RR2 10 9 8 7 6 5 4 3

www.andrewsmcmeel.com

Book design by Holly Camerlinck
Illustrations by Kevin Brimmer

Certified Chain of Custody
SUSTAINABLE FORESTRY INITIATIVE
60% Certified Fiber Sourcing and
40% Post-Consumer Recycled

www.sfiprogram.org

The SFI label only applies to the text stock.

ATTENTION: SCHOOLS AND BUSINESSES
Andrews McMeel books are available at quantity discounts with
bulk purchase for educational, business, or sales promotional
use. For information, please write to: Special Sales Department,
Andrews McMeel Publishing, LLC, 1130 Walnut Street,
Kansas City, Missouri 64106.

Stupid
American
History

BETTER THAN THE BEST

History books have idolized our founding fathers to such a degree that a lot of people believe they were perfect. Simply by looking at the first line of the Constitution you'll find that they weren't perfect——and they especially weren't *more* perfect. The first line of the preamble to the Constitution reads, "We the people of the United States, in order to form a more perfect union." If something is perfect it's, well, perfect——it can't be *more* perfect. Ask any English teacher, and they will tell you that "more perfect" ain't good English.

ANDREW JACKSON'S WIFE, RACHEL, WAS THE ONLY FIRST LADY WHO SMOKED A PIPE.

BETTER LATE THAN NEVER

General Andrew "Old Hickory" Jackson [he got his nickname because he was as hard as old hickory] was victorious over the invading British Army intent on seizing New Orleans during the War of 1812. The infamous Battle of New Orleans was an enormous boost, not necessarily to the war effort, but to the future career of Andrew Jackson. Jackson used his war hero status during his biggest battle ever——the battle to become the seventh president of the United States [1829—1837]. But was the Battle of New Orleans even an important battle? Not really. The war was already over before the Battle of New Orleans began. The Treaty of Ghent, which officially ended the War of 1812, had been signed on December 24, 1814; the Battle of New Orleans took place on January 8, 1815.

HAVING THE LAST WORD

What a man decides to have put on his tombstone says a lot about what was important in his life. One would think that a man like Thomas Jefferson might need several tombstones to cover all the accomplishments of which he was proud. Surprisingly, the inscription that Jefferson personally wrote left out a few key things. His tombstone reads: "Here was buried Thomas Jefferson, author of the Declaration of American Independence, of the Statute of Virginia for Religious Freedom, and Father of the University of Virginia." You'll notice that he doesn't mention that he was the second vice president of the United States or even that he was the third president.

A TOWN BY ANY OTHER NAME

When the Pilgrims finally landed and settled in Plymouth, Massachusetts, in 1620 [after having originally been dumped in Provincetown, Massachusetts, because the crew of the *Mayflower* was tired of their complaining], they named the city Plymouth because they had set sail from Plymouth, England. It makes perfect sense and is widely believed, but it's not true. The city was already named Plymouth. In 1614, Captain John Smith mapped out the northeast coast of North America starting from Jamestown, Virginia, and he returned to England with a map on which most landmarks had, of course, Indian names. Smith asked Prince Charles to replace the "barbarous" Native American names with good old-fashioned English ones, and His Royal Highness obliged. When Prince Charles came to the Native American name "Accomack" on the map, he decided to change it to Plymouth. The fact that the *Mayflower* set sail from Plymouth, England, and landed in Plymouth, Massachusetts, is just a fun fluke in American history.

DOUBLEDAY DOUBLE PLAY

When asked, "Who invented baseball?" most people would answer, "Abner Doubleday," and most people would be wrong. Baseball was invented in England [gasp!]. It was first named and described in 1744 in *A Little Pretty Pocket Book*, which was reprinted in the United States in 1762. So how did Abner Doubleday get credit for inventing a game that had been around for nearly a hundred years? It was a propaganda campaign. The Major League's executive board, wanting to score a home run by claiming baseball had been invented in America, commissioned a report on the game's origin in 1907. In this report, baseball was first credited with being the brainchild of Civil War general and hero Abner Doubleday in Cooperstown, New York, in 1839. Even though Doubleday never mentioned inventing baseball in his diaries, or the fact that he never visited Cooperstown. Makes you wonder about the origins of apple pie and Chevrolet now, doesn't it?

BASES LOADED

So who should get credit for inventing baseball? Most authorities now agree that Alexander Cartwright, a Manhattan bookseller, should get the credit for inventing the modern game of baseball. In 1842 he founded the Knickerbocker Baseball Club, named after the Knickerbocker Fire Engine Company, for which he was a volunteer. Cartwright drew the first diagram of the diamond-shaped field and the rules of the modern game are based on bylaws his team created. He was finally inducted into the Baseball Hall of Fame in 1938.

IN 1989, GEORGE HERBERT WALKER BUSH
WAS THE FIRST VICE PRESIDENT ELECTED TO THE
OFFICE OF THE PRESIDENCY SINCE MARTIN VAN BUREN
IN 1836.

BEDFORD FALLS

The warm-hearted fantasy *It's a Wonderful Life*, produced and directed by Frank Capra for Liberty Films, was nominated for five Oscars [without winning any] and is recognized by the American Film Institute as one of the 100 best American films ever made. It is placed number one on their list of the most inspirational American films of all time. But when it was first released on December 20, 1946, it was considered a flop. The movie cost $2,300,000 and grossed only about $2,000,000 during its initial release——less than half of what Liberty Films expected.

ON JUNE 28, 1836, JAMES MADISON'S LAST WORDS WERE "I ALWAYS TALK BETTER LYING DOWN."

LOSING HIS MARBLES

In April 1841, Vice President John Tyler was on his knees playing marbles when he was informed that William Henry Harrison had died, and he was now president of the United States. At that time, marbles was a very popular game for both children and grown-ups.

LET FREEDOM RING

On July 8, 1776, the grand peal of the Liberty Bell alerted citizens that the country they lived in was now independent, while the founding fathers read to them the Declaration of Independence that freed them from the tyranny of British rule. But the story just doesn't ring true. It's true that the bell was hanging in the Philadelphia statehouse at the time, but no one rang it. Why would they? It had a huge crack in it from a forging error and, at that time, was not a symbol of freedom or liberty. The name Liberty Bell wasn't adopted until 1839 in a pamphlet entitled *The Liberty Bell, by Friends of Freedom*, where it symbolized the liberty of black slaves, not the independence of white Americans from Britain. Until that time it was called the State House Bell——because it hung in the statehouse.

STAY TUNED

Television was first demonstrated to the general public at the 1939 New York World's Fair. But not everyone who tuned in was turned on. One critic from the *New York Times* remarked that television would never actually compete with radio because "people must sit and keep their eyes glued on a screen; the average American family hasn't the time for it."

BIRDS OF A FEATHER

Confederate General Richard Ewell was an odd-looking fellow with a beak-like nose and a bald head that he would cock to one side when he was speaking. Because he had lost a leg in a previous battle, he hopped around camp like a parakeet. Ewell fought bravely at Gettysburg, but he had such a nervous disposition that he found it difficult to sleep in a normal position and would curl around a stool instead of lying in his cot. He had convinced himself that he had some mysterious internal "disease," and his diet consisted almost entirely of frumenty, hulled wheat boiled in milk and sweetened with sugar. It was also reported from camp guards that Ewell would sit in his tent for hours alone——quietly chirping to himself.

Apparently more Catholics attended Mass during Prohibition than any time in American history——because the production of legal sacramental wine increased by hundreds of thousands of gallons during that time.

ANOTHER BRIQUETTE
IN THE WALL

What do you get when you combine the foremost American inventor and America's foremost car manufacturer? Would you believe the charcoal briquette? Thomas Edison and Henry Ford are credited with making, from sawdust and glue from Ford's factory floor and Edison's creative wizardry, the infamous barbecue fuel. They made it, but they got the idea from someone else: Ellsworth B. A. Zwoyer, who invented, designed, and patented the original briquette in 1897. The mystery as to why Ford and Edison decided to make their own charcoal briquettes has a simple solution——they took the idea from one of their friends, Ellsworth Zwoyer.

WHAT COMES AROUND

As President John Adams and his wife, Abigail, traveled home from Philadelphia [then the capital] to Braintree, Massachusetts, they passed through Newark, New Jersey, and the town celebrated the occasion with pomp and ceremony. But not everyone enjoyed seeing the Federalist president, especially Republican Luther Baldwin, who stumbled out of John Burnet's dram shop and stared drunkenly at the commotion. Hearing the sixteen-gun salute and knowing Baldwin's hatred of the president, one customer exclaimed, "There goes the president and they are firing at his ass." To which Baldwin chimed, "I don't care if they fire through his ass!" With that remark, Baldwin was immediately arrested under the new Alien and Sedition laws [similar to the modern Patriot Act] for uttering "seditious words tending to defame the President and Government of the United States." Baldwin was fined, assessed court costs, and sent to a federal jail until he made financial amends.

RUMORS OF MY DEATH HAVE BEEN EXAGGERATED

In 1800, newspapers across the United States printed the sad news that Vice President Thomas Jefferson had died at Monticello [his estate in Virginia] after a brief illness. From the moment the article was first printed in a Baltimore paper on June 30 and for an entire week some people were grief stricken, some were doubtful about the story, and some, mainly Jefferson's enemies, were hopeful. It turned out that Thomas Jefferson had died as reported, but it wasn't Thomas Jefferson the author of the Declaration of Independence——it was one of Thomas Jefferson's slaves who shared the same name. It was twenty-six years before Thomas Jefferson died in 1826——on July 4.

GEORGE HERBERT WALKER BUSH IS THE ONLY PRESIDENT WITH FOUR NAMES.

THE BLACK AND RED OF IT ALL

On January 8, 1835, the United States under President Andrew Jackson, for the first and only time, completely paid off its national debt [well, actually we still owed $33,733.05, but who's counting?]. This was accomplished through the sale of public lands in the West. The country was debt free for only a short time, and then it rapidly went millions of dollars into the red.

On May 16, 1974, Richard Kleindienst, John Mitchell's successor as attorney general after the Watergate scandal, pled guilty to a misdemeanor charge of failing to accurately testify before a Senate committee. Kleindienst is the first attorney general ever convicted of a crime.

DON'T FLIP YOUR WHIG

When the Whig party nominated Zachary Taylor as its presidential candidate in early June 1848, they sent him a letter notifying him of their choice, and he sent the letter back. Why? Because at that time, recipients of letters paid the postage, not the person sending the letter. In fact, the first stamp was issued only one year before Taylor's nomination, but the practice of recipient-paid postage still continued. Because Taylor was extremely popular as one of the heroes of the Mexican-American War [I guess you could say he was a Big Whig], he received a great deal of fan mail for which he would have had to pay the postage. So he routinely returned all the mail he received, including the nomination. It wasn't until July that Taylor learned he was the official candidate for the Whig Party. He went on to become president in 1849 and was the last Whig ever elected.

THE RIDE OF YOUR LIFE

When most Americans think about a heroic horseback ride to warn citizens of a British invasion, they think of Paul Revere. But Revere only rode nineteen miles before he was captured. So why do we remember him, and not the truly heroic 345-mile ride by Israel Bissell? Who? Bissell, a twenty-three-year-old postal rider, rode four days and six hours [April 19, 1775—April 23, 1775] from Boston to Philadelphia, warning the citizens of each town he rode through by shouting, "To arms, to arms. The war has begun." He was so underappreciated for his bravery that in several historical documents his first name was inaccurately listed as Trail.

UNTIL 1900, THE STATE OF RHODE ISLAND HAD TWO CAPITALS,
ONE AT PROVIDENCE AND THE OTHER AT NEWPORT.

GRANT YOUR WISHES

Some people, mainly Republicans, charged John Kennedy with nepotism when he asked his brother Bobby to serve as attorney general. But the king of keeping it in the family was Republican President Ulysses S. Grant. Grant placed his father on the payroll as postmaster at Covington, Kentucky; his wife's brother-in-law James Casey was appointed collector of customs to the Port of New Orleans; another brother-in-law served as appraiser of customs in San Francisco; his cousin Silas Hudson was named a minister to Guatemala; and another brother-in-law was minister to Denmark. In all, nearly forty people associated with Grant, including thirteen relatives, benefited from "Grantism."

GEORGE WASHINGTON WAS THE FIRST AND ONLY PRESIDENT TO HAVE BEEN ELECTED BY A UNANIMOUS ELECTORAL VOTE.

A CHAMBER MUSICIAN

On January 23, 1978, Terry Kath, lead guitarist for the rock group Chicago, was playing around with a .38 revolver during a party. As a joke, he put the gun to his head and pulled the trigger. Kath, a gun enthusiast, then picked up a 9mm semi-automatic pistol and prepared to do the same thing but was asked by the party's host to stop. Kath deftly removed the gun's clip, reassured the host by saying, "Don't worry, it's not loaded," and proceeded to shoot himself in the head. Even though Kath had removed the magazine he had forgotten to unload the chamber and was killed instantly.

In 1908, the grandnephew of
Napoleon Bonaparte, Charles Joseph
Bonaparte, created the Bureau
of Investigation, which would later
become known as the FBI.

A SLAVE TO THE PAST

When they were boys, future Presidents Millard Fillmore and Andrew Johnson were indentured servants. An indentured servant is a laborer under contract to an employer for a specified period of time, usually three to seven years, in exchange for necessities such as food, drink, clothing, transportation, and lodging. The master basically owned the indentured servant, who had hardly any rights, until the term of the contract was met. Andrew Johnson was indentured to a tailor, and he ran away. The tailor placed an advertisement in the *Raleigh Gazette* [North Carolina], offering a reward of $10 for the capture and return of the future President Johnson. Fillmore served his master, a cloth maker, for several years and was able to purchase his freedom for $30. Sometimes I wonder if we would have been better off if they had stayed indentured servants.

OUT OF THE MOUTH OF ABE

It's a well-told story that President Abraham Lincoln once responded to complaints about the drinking habits of General Ulysses S. Grant by saying, "If I knew what brand he used, I'd send every other general in the field a barrel of it." It's a great story and really exemplifies Lincoln's sense of humor, but according to David Homer Bates's book *Lincoln Stories*, Lincoln's response when asked if he had ever made this infamous quip was that he never had said it. Well, at least he was honest.

A GRAHAM OF GOODNESS

Presbyterian minister Reverend Sylvester Graham developed the graham cracker in Bound Brook, New Jersey, in 1822, but it wasn't to complete the recipe for S'mores. In fact, it was created so that people wouldn't want s'more of anything——especially sex. Graham believed his cracker, along with bland foods and a strict vegetarian diet, could cure not only alcoholism but more important, sexual urges [which he believed to be the source of many maladies]. Graham's belief that eating pure foods created a purity of mind, spirit, and body influenced several people, including Dr. John Harvey Kellogg, the inventor of the corn flakes breakfast cereal.

In 1871, Tucson, Arizona, was the heart of the Wild West, and boasted 3,000 people, two doctors, a newspaper, a brewery, and several salons—— but just one bathtub.

A Vein Endeavor

Bloodletting, or bleeding, is now considered an antiquated, useless, and dangerous [sometimes deadly] form of medicine. A great deal of blood is drawn from the patient in the hope that it will balance the four humors of the body [black bile, yellow bile, phlegm, and blood] that were thought to control all bodily functions. Surprisingly, people still practiced bloodletting up into the twentieth century, as this ad from the 1905 Sears catalog proves: "Spring Bleeding Lance. The only practicable, safe and convenient instrument for bleeding on the market. Used almost exclusively by old school physicians for the purpose." Still, it sounds better than one of the other old school practices——leeches.

DON'T BE SUCH A BABY!

It's true that Dr. Benjamin Spock was an American pediatrician whose book *Baby and Child Care*, published in 1946, is one of publishing's best sellers of all time. But what's not true is the rumor that he was jailed for his anti-Vietnam point of view during the 1960s. Spock was arrested in 1968 and convicted on charges of conspiring to advise young men to avoid the draft, but he appealed the verdict, and his conviction was reversed the following year.

Before Spock's groundbreaking
childcare book was published,
John B. Watson's 1928 book
Psychological Care of Infant and Child
was used widely in American hospitals
and contained such stern advice as,
"Never kiss your children."

HI HOE, HI HOE

On December 25, 1790, twenty-five girls from an asylum in Paris, France, called the Saltpêtrière were sent to the Louisiana colony in America because there were so few women. By their action, the French government also hoped to lure Canadian settlers away from Indian mistresses.

SELLING YOURSELF SHORT

Henry John Heinz, president of the H. J. Heinz Company, was riding on an elevated railway in New York City in 1896 when he saw an "advertising card" for shoes that read "21 Styles." Heinz was taken with the idea of using a number to promote his company and started counting in his head the variety of products his company produced. He easily counted more than sixty but he kept coming back to the number 57. There was something special about the number seven. "Seven, seven," quoted E. D. McCafferty in his book *Henry J. Heinz: a Biography*. "There are so many illustrations of the psychological influence of that figure and of its alluring significance to people of all ages and races that '58 Varieties' or '59 Varieties' did not appeal at all to me as being equally strong." That's why "57 Varieties" is still the company's motto.

A SLAVE TO FASHION

We are led to believe, in our abbreviated versions of history, that all slave-holding states seceded from the Union during the Civil War, or else they gave up the practice of slavery. But that's just not true. Kentucky, Missouri, Maryland, and Delaware remained in the Union but continued to allow citizens to own slaves. They were referred to as "border states" and were joined by West Virginia when it was admitted to the Union in 1863 [after it split from the northwestern counties of Virginia after Virginia seceded from the Union]. Once again, this demonstrates that the Civil War was anything but black and white.

CURTAIN CALL

On June 13, 1932, twenty-four-year-old actress Peg Entwistle signed a contract for a one-picture deal with RKO Studios and reported early in July to shoot her part as "Hazel Cousins" in *Thirteen Women*. The film received poor feedback from test screenings, and the studio re-edited the film, greatly reducing Entwistle's screen time. On September 16, 1932, Entwistle climbed up the giant "H" in the famous Hollywood sign [which read Hollywoodland, at that time] and jumped to her death. In a cruel twist of fate, Entwistle's uncle opened a letter addressed to the dead actress from the Beverly Hills Playhouse, mailed the day before she jumped. The letter was an offer for Entwistle to play the lead role in a theatrical production in which her character commits suicide.

There were more than 46,000 write-in votes for Edward "Ted" Kennedy for U.S. senator in 1962. Which isn't stupid in and of itself——until you discover that the voters lived in Connecticut, while Kennedy was running in Massachusetts.

BEHIND EVERY GOOD MAN

On October 2, 1919, President Woodrow Wilson suffered a severe stroke, and he was soon bedridden and incapacitated. The president's wife, Edith Bolling Galt Wilson, did more than just take control of the president's recovery; she also took control of the presidency. She would bring important papers to her husband under the guise of explaining them to him, but what she was actually doing was making presidential decisions in his place. For the next six weeks, she was the true power behind the presidency, although she claimed, "I, myself, never made a single decision regarding the disposition of public affairs. The only decision that was mine was what was important and what was not." She has been labeled "the secret president" and even "the first female president of the United States." Mrs. Wilson was both criticized and ridiculed by many as the "presidentress" who was running a "petticoat government."

SUFFERING SUFFRAGETTE

There are two women who ran for president who shared a very unusual situation in history. Even though they ran for the office, they couldn't vote for themselves or anyone else, for that matter. Victoria Claflin Woodhull ran on the National Radical Reform ticket in 1872, and Belva Ann Bennett Lockwood ran on the National Equal Rights ticket in 1884 and 1888. Why could they run for the presidency but not vote in the election? Because both women ran before the Nineteenth Amendment to the Constitution was ratified in 1920——giving women the right to vote.

GETTING TO THE BOTTOM
OF THE CONSTITUTION

The Twenty-Fifth Amendment authorizing the vice president to take over the presidency if the president is temporarily incapacitated is relatively new, having been enacted in 1967. As of this printing, the amendment has been used only three times:

★ On July 13, 1985, President Ronald Reagan underwent surgery to remove cancerous polyps from his colon and Vice President George H. W. Bush took over the presidency.

★ On June 29, 2002, Vice President Dick Cheney temporarily took over the presidency when President George W. Bush had a colonoscopy that required sedation.

★ On July 21, 2007, President George W. Bush had to undergo the same procedure and Dick Cheney, once again, took over the Oval Office.

I'm glad the Twenty-Fifth Amendment filled in all the cracks in the transference of presidential powers.

STRANGE INTERLUDE

Future Pulitzer prize—winning playwright and Nobel laureate in literature Eugene O'Neill attended Princeton University during the 1907—1908 term, but he was kicked out after his freshman year. He was expelled, not only for poor grades, but also for allegedly being drunk and disorderly at a reception held by the university president, future President of the United States Woodrow Wilson.

Every U.S. president with a beard has
been a Republican. In case you're curious,
the five bearded presidents were
Abraham Lincoln, Ulysses S. Grant,
Rutherford Hayes, James Garfield, and
Benjamin Harrison.

THAT'S SORT OF WEIRD

On September 11, 2002, the first anniversary of the September 11 terrorist attacks, the numbers that popped up for the New York Lottery were 9-1-1. So what were the chances of those three numbers coming up on the anniversary of the attacks in the same city in which the attacks took place? Seems like it might be astronomical, but it's actually the same as any three-number combinations: 1 out of 1,000. Sorry, conspiracy theorists.

Notorious Wild West "peacekeeper"
James Butler "Wild Bill" Hickok
shot only two people while presiding
over Abilene, Texas; one of them was
another policeman.

JUST FOR THE RECORD

In the American lexicon there are some words that don't seem to make sense anymore because their original meanings have been lost. Take, for example, the use of the word "album" for a vinyl record. When records spun at 78 RPM, they could only hold four to five minutes of music per side. So you needed several records if you were listening to a symphony or an opera. The records were packaged in brown paper sleeves that fanned out from inside a leather-bound book that resembled a photo album. Soon, any long-playing record was called an album whether it came in a set or by itself.

DON'T HAVE A COW, MAN I

Mickey Mouse is usually a moral, upright do-gooder with a heart of gold. So why would one of his cartoons ever be banned? Well, one was in Ohio in 1932. The cartoon, *The Shindig,* showed Clarabelle Cow, the first cartoon in which she's identified by name, in the stable reading a book titled *Three Weeks.* So what's the big deal? For one, when her boyfriend Horace Horsecollar knocks on the door, Clarabelle gets up and dresses, so she was technically naked while she was reading the book. The second big deal was that *Three Weeks* was written by Elinor Glyn, a British novelist and scriptwriter who pioneered mass-market women's erotic fiction and also coined the use of the word "It" as a euphemism for sex appeal [1920s motion picture sex starlet Clara Bow was called "The It Girl"]. *Three Weeks* was deemed obscene, banned in Canada in 1907, and condemned by religious leaders in the United States. How it came to be used in a Walt Disney cartoon remains a mystery to this day.

ALL IN THE FAMILY

George W. Bush is related to two former presidents: his father, George H. W. Bush [1989—1993], and his fourth cousin five times removed——Franklin Pierce, president from 1853 to 1857. Barbara Pierce Bush is the only woman in U.S. history to be the wife of one president, mother to another, and fourth cousin of another.

A NEEDLING RUMOR

You might not know the name Elizabeth Griscom Ross, but if I called her Betsy Ross, you'd say she's the woman who designed and sewed the first flag. But sewing the flag is a yarn created by Betsy's grandson, William Canby. Canby first mentioned the moment in March 1870 [thirty-six years after his grandmother had died] before a meeting of the Historical Society of Pennsylvania, claiming Betsy told him about the first flag while on her deathbed when he was eleven. There is proof that Betsy had sewn "ship's colors" for the Pennsylvania Navy in May 1777 but nothing whatsoever that supports one of the most beloved rumors in American history.

After Canby's death, a book called *The Evolution of the American Flag* was published in 1909, and it used Canby's claim of the Betsy Ross story as fact. The misinformation spread from there.

NEVER A TWAIN SHALL MEET

There are a few things most people know about Mark Twain. One, he is one of the greatest American authors in history. Two, his real name was Samuel Langhorne Clemens. And three, he got his name from the traditional call of Mississippi boaters who announced "Mark Twain" [the second mark on a leadline used to calculate the river's depth] that indicated two fathoms [twelve feet]——a safe depth for boats to travel. The first two are correct but Clemens didn't get his name from a nautical term——he Shanghaid it. Captain Isaiah Sellers, a river news correspondent for the New Orleans *Picayune*, used the name Mark Twain first. When Sellers died in 1863, Clemens began using the name as his own. He explained this personally in a letter, stating, "as he [Sellers] could no longer need that signature, I laid violent hands upon it without asking permission of the proprietor's remains. That is the history of the nom de plume I bear."

MARX ON OUR PAST

The Pilgrims have come to symbolize the heart of the American spirit. But when they first arrived in Plymouth in 1620, they established their community in a most un-American way——they were communists. Under the Mayflower Compact, the Pilgrims attempted to create a just and equal society; whatever they produced was put into a common warehouse, with each individual getting one equal share. All the land, buildings, and end product were owned communally. How well did it work? Well, you don't see too many Pilgrims walking around these days, do you? Actually, it only worked for a year or two, and then they changed to that most American economic structure——capitalism.

LEAVE THE LIGHT ON FOR ME

Most cities have what is commonly referred to as a red-light district; a place where prostitutes ply their trade. So why is it called a red-light district? The usually agreed-upon answer is that when railway workers visited "women of the night," they would hang their red lanterns outside the brothels so they could be found if they were needed.

ROBERT McNAMARA, U.S. SECRETARY OF DEFENSE FROM 1961 TO 1968, HAD A VERY STRANGE MIDDLE NAME: STRANGE. HE GOT HIS MIDDLE NAME "STRANGE" FROM HIS MOTHER'S MAIDEN NAME.

THE FIRST REAL
AMERICAN PRESIDENT

The first president to be born a citizen of the United States was number eight, Martin Van Buren. He was born on December 5, 1782, six years after the signing of the Constitution. Because all previous presidents had been born before the American Revolution, they were actually British subjects.

CIVIL WAR UNION GENERAL WILLIAM TECUMSEH SHERMAN,
NAMED AT BIRTH FOR THE NOTORIOUS INDIAN CHIEF,
ADDED WILLIAM AS HIS FIRST NAME.

THE PEANUT NUT

One of the most shining examples of sibling embarrassment for any president had to be Jimmy Carter's brother, Billy. Billy personified the beer-gutted, beer-swigging hillbilly stereotype, and he was consistently making the news. Once it was for judging and participating in a world championship belly flop competition; another time he even urinated on an airport tarmac while awaiting a delegation of Libyans he was hosting. He even went so far as to accept a $220,000 loan from Libya [at that time, an enemy of the United States], which propelled him once again into the spotlight as the key subject in a federal investigation.

WHEN BILLY CARTER WAS ASKED WHY HIS BROTHER JIMMY
DIDN'T TRY TO CONTROL HIS BEHAVIOR, BILLY SAID,
"I'D TELL HIM TO KISS MY ASS."

A CIVIL UNION

One would think that the Puritans believed in the purity and sanctity of marriage——and they did; they just didn't think the marriage ceremony should be religious in nature. In fact, in 1647 the Puritans in New England actually outlawed the preaching of wedding ceremonies [the year before they mandated that all wedding ceremonies be conducted by a civil magistrate]. The rationale was that the Puritans believed marriage was a government institution, not a religious one. Before the end of the century, however, the Puritans vowed that it was all right for weddings to take place in a church and allowed both ministers and justices of the peace to perform the ceremony.

BAD TIMING

Financial executive and the builder of the Empire State Building, John Jacob Raskob, wrote an article for the *Ladies' Home Journal* entitled "Everybody Ought to Be Rich"——just a month before the stock market crashed in October 1929.

A LEGEND IN HIS OWN MIND

Legendary Wild West gunman Bat Masterson [William Barclay Masterson, 1853—1921] has been considered a notorious killer for years. The stories of his gun-slinging skills are legendary, and legends they are. It has been reported that Masterson killed twenty-seven men, but according to Robert DeArment's thoroughly researched biography, he is only credited with killing one person.

SHOOTING BLANKS

It is common knowledge that the military purposely puts saltpeter in the food of enlisted men to curb their sexual appetite. It's well known, all right——but it's a well-known falsehood. There's no proof that potassium nitrate [known as saltpeter] has any effect on the libido, one way or the other. One theory as to why this rumor started is simply because the name saltpeter sounds like it might have some negative effect on a service member.

TOUGH LOVE

In colonial Connecticut, the adage "spare the rod and spoil the child" was taken seriously. George Brinley's book *The Laws of Connecticut* shows just how seriously they took this advice to heart. "If any Childe or Children above fifteen years old, and of sufficient understanding, shall Curse or Smite their natural Father or Mother, he or they shall be put to death, unless it can be sufficiently testified, that the Parents have been unchristianly negligent in the education of such Children."

LET'S MAKE A DEAL

Here's how it went: Spiro Agnew resigned after bribery allegations had surfaced. Richard Nixon appointed Gerald Ford to take Agnew's place as vice president. When Richard Nixon resigned after Watergate, Gerald Ford took over as president of the United States, and he appointed Nelson Rockefeller as his vice president. Shortly after taking the reins of power, Gerald Ford granted Richard Nixon a full pardon for any crimes he may have committed in the Watergate case. Then Ford lobbied Congress to award former President Nixon $850,000 to cover expenses while he made the transition from the White House to civilian life——a compromise was reached and Nixon was given $200,000.

Ford considered the sum of $850,000 to be fair because the Presidential Transition Act of 1963 provides ex-presidents [who complete their full term in office] funds not to exceed $900,000 to cover their expenses during the six-month transition period.

A Big Wig

Beautiful elegant dresses, silk stockings, the newest fashions from France, and high-heeled boots to die for were the customary clothes of the governor of New York who served from 1702 to 1708. What's the big deal, you might ask? Well, he wasn't a female——he was a notorious transvestite named Lord Cornbury [Edward Hyde] and not surprisingly a favorite of Queen Anne. Lord Cornbury had long, luscious nails, wore his hair in the most fashionable coif, and was frequently seen parading around the grounds of the governor's mansion. And you thought politicians today were a real drag.

HERBERT HOOVER WAS THE ONLY PRESIDENT TO TURN
HIS ENTIRE SALARY OVER TO CHARITY.

GOING DOWN

In 1975 Congress modernized the elevators in the Capitol building, changing them from the old-fashioned manually operated ones to the new push-button type. So the need for elevator operators was eliminated, right? This is Congress, remember. It was decided that the elevator operators would stay on the government payroll and continue their new duties——pushing the buttons on automatic elevators.

SNOWFLAKE, ARIZONA, GOT ITS NAME FROM TWO EARLY SETTLERS:
ERASTUS SNOW AND WILLIAM J. FLAKE.

REPRESENTIN'

The first African American elected to the U.S. Senate was Hiram Rhodes Revels, who represented Mississippi in 1870 and 1871, during Reconstruction. In an ironic twist, the man who occupied the seat before Revel was Jefferson Davis, president of the Confederacy.

In 1792, New York Governor George Clinton basically stole the governor's race from John Jay, Alexander Hamilton's handpicked candidate, simply by declaring the votes of three counties invalid and announcing himself the winner. Clinton was New York's first and longest-serving governor, having been re-elected six times.

A BAD FIRST ACT

Most Americans imagine that our founding fathers were big on liberty, free speech, and all that other stuff——but not during the administration of John Adams. In 1798, Adams signed four bills into law called the Alien and Sedition Acts that were supposed to protect American interests against foreign intrusion during our undeclared naval war with France. One of the bills, the Sedition Act, made it a crime to publish "false, scandalous, and malicious writing against" the government or its officials. So the Federalists in Congress could jail anyone who criticized anything the government did. More than twenty Republican newspaper editors were indicted and most were sent to jail.

Thomas Jefferson was vice president during the enforcement of the Alien and Sedition Acts, and he stopped signing his letters out of fear that postal clerks would search his mail looking for evidence to charge him with treason.

REMEMBER IT CORRECTLY

There are a few things that come to mind when the state of Texas is mentioned: big hats, longhorns, and the Battle of the Alamo. When the Mexican army was taken by surprise at the short-lived [approximately eighteen minutes] Battle of San Jacinto, "Remember the Alamo" was the battle cry of the Americans. But what was the Battle of the Alamo? Did Mexican forces invade the United States? No, it was just the opposite. Mexican President Antonio López de Santa Anna was attempting to retake the province after an army of Texan settlers and adventurers had driven Mexican troops off their own land.

IN CONGRESS ASSEMBLED

The Continental Congress, which met in three incarnations from 1774 to 1789, was very different from the Congress we have today. They actually got things done. But despite having to deal with highly important matters [establishing a country isn't as easy as it sounds], they still had time for trivial matters——and I'm not talking about giving post offices celebrity names. During one session, the Continental Congress spent hours debating whether one James Whitehead should receive $64 in compensation for feeding British prisoners; they decided in his favor. Then there was the debate over paying a wagon master $222.60 for transporting army supplies to Dobbs Ferry, New York, and Cambridge, Massachusetts. After several hours of heated debate, they decided to pay him, too.

OFF KEY

Contrary to what most people believe, Francis Scott Key didn't write the song *The Star-Spangled Banner*. He wrote a poem called *Defense of Fort McHenry* from which the lyrics of *The Star-Spangled Banner* were taken.

RICHARD M. NIXON WAS THE FIRST PRESIDENT TO BE NOMINATED FOR A GRAMMY AWARD. HE WAS NOMINATED FOR BEST SPOKEN WORD AWARD FOR AN ALBUM MADE FROM THE SOUNDTRACK OF HIS TELEVISION INTERVIEW WITH DAVID FROST.

SUB-STANDARD

Submarine warfare is usually thought of in terms of German U2s and the well-documented battles during World War II. But the first submarine used in warfare came much earlier. In fact, the Americans used the first submarine during the War of Independence. A sub was invented by Yale graduate David Bushnell, and was used only once. The small wooden-framed, oval-shaped vessel [called "the Turtle"] only had enough room for one person and enough oxygen for a half-hour submersion. On September 6, 1776, First Sergeant Ezra Lee propelled the small submarine close to the British warship HMS *Eagle* and attempted to attach a bomb to the hull of the ship with an iron screw. Unfortunately, the ship had a copper-sheathed hull that the screw could not penetrate. Even though George Washington was an enthusiastic supporter of the Turtle and submarine technology, the Continental Congress cut off all funding for the project.

THE GOOD OLE DAYS— PART I

Most people think our forefathers were gracious and eloquent men of class and honor——not like the members of Congress we have today. Well, I hate to burst the bubble, but here are verbatim excerpts from the *Historical Summary of Conduct Cases in the House of Representatives* by the Committee on Standards of Official Conduct:

★ Representative Matthew Lyon [VT] [1798] "Disorderly behavior" [spat on Rep. Roger Griswold after an exchange of insults], [Jan. 30, 1798]; charge added of "gross indecency of language in his defense before this House" [Feb. 8, 1798].

★ Representative Roger Griswold [CT] and Representative Matthew Lyon [VT] "Disorderly behavior" [Rep. Griswold assaulted Representative Lyon with a "stout cane" on the House floor before the House was in session and Rep. Lyon responded by attacking Representative Griswold with fireplace tongs], [Feb. 15, 1798].

PEAL AND CRACK

The Liberty Bell was cast at the Whitechapel Bell Foundry in London, England, and delivered to Philadelphia in late August to early September 1752 via the ship *Hibernia*. In March of 1753, the bell was hung from temporary scaffolding in the square outside the State House, and it cracked when it was first rung. It was repaired and recast several times, but the crack kept coming back.

Eli Whitney technically didn't invent
the cotton gin; he borrowed the idea
from an earlier invention and improved
upon it. The "gin" part of the name
was short for "engine."

ETYMOLOGICALLY SPEAKING

During the debate over the Missouri Compromise of 1820, Felix Walker, congressman from Buncombe County, North Carolina, stood up in the House and said he wanted "to make a speech for Buncombe" even though the matter up for debate was irrelevant to Walker's district. His rant was so long-winded and disjointed that a new word, "buncombe" [later respelled "bunkum"], was coined. It was defined as "Speech-making for the gratification of constituents, or to gain public applause" or "nonsense," and from that word we get the more modern derivative, "bunk."

DEAL OR NO DEAL

A loyalist spy learned that George Washington and his small Continental Army had secretly crossed the Delaware River earlier on the day after Christmas in 1776 and were headed toward Trenton, New Jersey. The spy arrived at the home of merchant Abraham Hunt where the leader of the Hessian army, Colonel Johann Rall, was drinking and playing cards. The colonel refused to break from his game of cards and demanded the spy hand over the written message, which he promptly put in his vest pocket without reading. Colonel Rall was awakened the next day to the sound of musket fire and, having no time to organize or rally his troops, suffered a crushing defeat at the hands of Washington's army. He also suffered two wounds that led to his eventual death the following day and gave the Continental Army its first victory over the British.

GRAND OLD FLAG

When Vermont and Kentucky came into the Union on March 4, 1791, and June 1, 1792, respectively, Congress altered the standard flag of thirteen stars and thirteen stripes and adopted a flag of fifteen stars and fifteen stripes. In 1818, after Tennessee, Ohio, Louisiana, and Indiana joined the Union, Congress knew that the flag would soon look like a quilt if they kept adding stripes for each new state. They decided to revert back to the original thirteen stripes and to simply add a star for every new state.

Andrew Jackson was the first president
to be handed a baby to kiss during
his campaign. He refused to kiss
the infant, and instead he handed the
baby over to his secretary of war.

No, No, Sirhan Sirhan

On May 10, 1982, convicted killer Sirhan Sirhan told a parole board, "I sincerely believe that if Robert Kennedy were alive today, I believe he would not countenance singling me out for this kind of treatment. I think he would be among the first to say that, however horrible the deed I committed fourteen years ago was, that it should not be the cause for denying me equal treatment under the laws of this country." Sirhan is serving life in prison for the June 5, 1968, assassination of Robert Kennedy.

**THE FIRST CHILD BORN ON THE *MAYFLOWER*
WAS NAMED OCEANUS HOPKINS.**

CABIN FEVER

President William Henry Harrison, who served only thirty-two days in office before his death from blood poisoning complicated by pneumonia and jaundice, campaigned as a candidate of humble beginnings. He was touted as having been born in a log cabin, and Harrison himself made references to his "log cabin home." But he was actually born in a two-and-a-half-story red brick mansion located on a large plantation on the James River in Virginia. The only log cabin to which he could lay claim was one that happened to be on his property and that one he most definitely never lived in.

No Bull

There is a much believed but erroneous story that Sitting Bull killed Lieutenant Colonel George Armstrong Custer during the Battle of the Little Bighorn on June 25, 1876. Sitting Bull didn't fight in the battle because he was simply too old at the time, but he did serve as his tribe's holy man. His earlier premonitions that all his enemies would be delivered into his hands came true after Custer's Last Stand.

Abraham Lincoln was the first and only president to receive a patent. Patent #6469 was a very complex device, much like car safety air-bags of today, that incorporated chambers of air. But Lincoln's invention was much grander and was designed to help heavy ships pass through shallow water.

CUT TO THE CHASE

In 1903, when the Gillette Company started selling safety razors with disposable blades, they were shocked when hundreds of men complained that the razors didn't work. It was soon discovered that the stubby disgruntled customers weren't removing the wrapping from around the blades before they put them into the razor.

American author Sherwood Anderson
died in Panama at the age of sixty-four
from peritonitis. The infection resulted
when the author accidentally swallowed
a piece of a toothpick embedded
in a martini olive.

DOESN'T FALL FAR FROM THE TREE

When one thinks of outrageous American folk heroes it doesn't take long for the names Paul Bunyan and Johnny Appleseed to pop up. Johnny Appleseed was a real person, but old Paul was a myth. Johnny Appleseed, born John Chapman [1774—1845], was an eccentric American nurseryman who introduced the apple to large parts of mainly Ohio, but also to Indiana and Illinois. Appleseed planted orchards and then turned their care over to neighbors who sold the apples and gave some of the profit to Appleseed. He would usually give it all away to charity. The image of him going barefoot is true——he never wore shoes even in winter——and it's possible that he wore a pot on his head because Appleseed remained a wanderer his entire life and carried all his meager belongings with him.

EVERY VOTE COUNTS

Before he died on October 18, 1931, Thomas Edison, "The Wizard of Menlo Park," held 1,093 U.S. patents. His first patent, granted in 1868, was for a vote counter intended to speed up the election process in Congress. Members of Congress, however, rejected the invention because they felt that, somehow, slowly tabulating votes was to their advantage.

A correspondent for the *New York Tribune*
who reported on politics in Europe
during the Civil War later became
infamous not as a newspaperman but as
the father of modern communism——
Karl Marx.

LOOK AT THE FLIP SIDE

Even though American money bears the motto "In God We Trust," which Treasury Secretary Salmon P. Chase had placed on the two-cent coin in 1864, not everyone has thought it an enlightened move. In 1907, President Theodore Roosevelt wrote to a friend saying, "It seems to me eminently unwise to cheapen such a motto by use on coins, just as it would be to cheapen it by use on postage stamps, or in advertisements." However, the courts have consistently upheld the use of the motto even though it has historically had opposition from constitutionalists [citing the First Amendment, "Congress shall make no law respecting an establishment of religion"].

ON JULY 30, 1956, PRESIDENT DWIGHT D. EISENHOWER
DECLARED "IN GOD WE TRUST" THE NATIONAL MOTTO
OF THE UNITED STATES.

GOING OFF HALF-COCKED

Robert Shurtleff [1760—1827] was a former indentured servant who enlisted in the Continental Army in 1782 and fought with the Fourth Massachusetts. Fellow soldiers gave Shurtleff the nickname Molly because of his inability to grow facial hair. Shurtleff was treated for a wound to the head but didn't tell the doctor about being shot in the thigh and tried to treat the wound personally. After being struck down with a fever, it was soon discovered that facial hair wasn't the only thing "Molly" hadn't grown——you see, Robert Shurtleff was actually a woman named Deborah Sampson. Sampson was discharged in 1783 and was the only woman to officially fight in the Revolutionary War. She was given a small pension, and, in 1802, she became one of the first American women to speak on a lecture tour. In 1838 Congress granted her heirs a full military pension.

THE ORIGINAL BENEDICT ARNOLD

How did the best general and most accomplished leader in the Continental Army become America's best known traitor? It started when the Continental Congress passed over Benedict Arnold for promotion even though if it hadn't been for his heroic contributions to the American Revolution we would all speak with an English accent. Arnold became despondent with what he believed was an affront to his honor and accomplishments [other generals took credit for a number of his deeds]. Then Congress investigated his accounts because of his personal debts, and he became the target of political adversaries. He was charged with corruption, and he opposed America's new alliance with France. So when he was given command of the American fort at West Point, New York, he had had enough and decided to change sides.

UP, UP, AND AWAY

It is sometimes reported that one year after Charles Lindbergh flew solo across the Atlantic Ocean in May 1927, Amelia Earhart became the first woman to do the same. Well, she did fly across the Atlantic in June 1928 but only as a passenger——she wasn't trained to fly on "instruments" and did not pilot the aircraft. When interviewed after landing, she said, "I was just baggage, like a sack of potatoes." She added, " . . . maybe someday I'll try it alone." And in May 1932 she did just that.

To her credit, in January 1935, Amelia Earhart became the first person to fly solo from Honolulu, Hawaii, to Oakland, California.

IN 1875, JAMES STEPHEN HOGG, THE FIRST NATIVE-BORN
TEXAN TO BECOME THE STATE'S GOVERNOR,
NAMED HIS DAUGHTER: IMA.

A TALL TALE

In 1869, while digging a well at an upstate New York farm just outside the town of Cardiff, workers found what appeared to be the petrified body of a man, but not just any man——a ten-foot-tall giant. When New York cigar maker George Hull, who had hired the workers, found out about their discovery, he began touring with the petrified body, which was known as the Cardiff Giant. He charged people 50 cents to see it. P. T. Barnum, who knew a good thing when he saw it, offered to buy the giant from Hull, and when Hull refused, he simply created his own giant and put it on display. He then sued Hull, declaring the original to be a fake. During the trial, Hull admitted the giant was an elaborate hoax, carved from gypsum and washed with sulfuric acid to make it look old. He created the hoax for two reasons: first, because he had an argument with a fundamentalist preacher concerning the "giants in the Earth" mentioned in the Bible; and, second, to make a bunch of money off the rubes of the Earth.

IN 1938, *TIME* MAGAZINE NAMED AS ITS MAN OF THE YEAR—
ADOLF HITLER.

THE END OF HIS ROPE

In 1872, criminals Patrick Morrissey, convicted of stabbing his mother to death, and Jack Gaffney were hanged by the neck until dead by the sheriff of Erie County, New York, who had the nickname The Buffalo Hangman. In 1885, the notorious hangman was referred to by another name, President Grover Cleveland.

Richard Nixon was the only person ever elected twice to both the office of president and the office of vice president. He also holds the less distinguished honor of being the only president ever to resign.

HOW TO AFFORD A FORD

We've all heard the infamous remark made by Henry Ford concerning the variety of colors for his Model T Ford: "Any color so long as it's black." But what most people don't know is that the car originally was painted green with a red stripe. However, it was only after an engineer discovered that black paint dried faster and therefore would speed up the assembly line process [it was cheaper, too] that Ford made the decision to paint all of his cars black.

NO ONE KNOWS WHAT CHRISTOPHER COLUMBUS REALLY LOOKED LIKE BECAUSE HE NEVER SAT FOR A PAINTING.

WASHINGTON'S EMBARRASSING
DISCHARGE

It's highly likely that the father of our country wasn't able to father a child by anybody. Even though George Washington claimed that he always wanted children, he and Martha never conceived. Martha, who had four children in seven years during her previous marriage, obviously wasn't at fault, so that leaves only one possibility: Washington had a monumental problem.

John Kennedy, at age forty-three, was not the youngest president of the United States. The youngest president was Theodore Roosevelt at forty-two. Kennedy, however, was the youngest man to be elected president——Roosevelt became president after McKinley died from an assassin's bullet on September 14, 1901.

NOT WHOLE CLOTH

One thing about the Declaration of Independence that isn't widely known is that Jefferson had to present the document to Congress for approval. Congress debated the document and, of course, made changes. In total, Congress made eighty-six revisions to Jefferson's masterpiece, eliminating 480 of his words. The most striking changes were that Congress removed all references to "the execrable commerce"——slavery.

THAT'S SNOT A GOOD NAME!

In 1962 the city council of Burleson, Texas, officially changed the name of Town Creek to Little Booger Creek. In 2001, when city managers wanted to apply for a federal grant for a creek-side hike and bike trail, they decided to change the name back to Town Creek so the paperwork wouldn't have a "booger" on it.

No American president has been an only child. Although, technically, Franklin D. Roosevelt had a younger half brother, Gerald Ford had four half brothers and two half sisters, and Bill Clinton has one younger half brother.

Tag, You're It!

There's a myth that circulated for years concerning government dog tags issued to United States Army personnel during World War II. This particularly morbid myth concerns the notches on both sides of the tags. It is rumored that the notches were placed between the teeth of a dead soldier, and then the mouth was kicked shut, ensuring the proper identification of the corpse. But the real answer is that the notches are there to hold the tag in place on the embossing machine. The new dog tags, which use a different embossing machine, don't have the notches.

You Say Tomato and I Say Tomato

It wasn't until the early 1800s that Americans began eating tomatoes, even though they are native to North America. It was believed that they were poisonous, because the tomato is related to the sometimes deadly Nightshade family. However, tomatoes were grown as decorative plants and commonly referred to as "love apples." Thomas Jefferson was a fan of the tomato [or "tomatas," as he called them in his journal] and grew them abundantly in his garden despite their unpopularity. Thomas Mann Randolph, Jefferson's son-in-law, in his 1824 speech before the Albemarle Agricultural Society, mentioned that tomatoes were relatively unknown ten years earlier, but by 1824 everyone was eating them because it was believed they "kept one's blood pure in the heat of summer."

DETAILS, DETAILS, DETAILS

President Martin Van Buren wrote his autobiography during 1862, the last year of his life, finally dictating it shortly before he died. But for some reason, Van Buren overlooked one aspect of his life——the fact that he had been married. He never mentioned his wife, Hannah Hoes, in the book at all.

SAMUEL MUDD, THE DOCTOR WHO TREATED THE BROKEN ANKLE OF LINCOLN'S ASSASSIN, JOHN WILKES BOOTH, RECEIVED A PRESIDENTIAL PARDON IN 1869 BY ULYSSES S. GRANT. CONTRARY TO SOME BELIEFS, THE PHRASE "YOUR NAME IS MUD!" DIDN'T ORIGINATE WITH DR. MUDD.

A TAXING SITUATION

Taxes and America have had a long past. In fact, the fight against "taxation without representation" helped drive us to become a free country in the first place. So when did we decide that taxing ourselves was okay? It started in 1861 when Congress passed the first income tax law as an emergency measure to fund the Civil War. In 1872, Congress repealed the income tax law but twenty-two years later, after complaints about excessive tariffs, Congress again approved an income tax. In 1895, the U.S. Supreme Court ruled that the income tax law was unconstitutional, and it was revoked. So what to do when a law is unconstitutional? Change the Constitution. Which is exactly what was done when the Sixteenth Amendment to the Constitution was enacted in 1913.

NOT IN A BOX, NOT WITH A FOX

Twenty-three New York publishers rejected Theodor Geisel's first book before one decided it was worth printing. *And To Think That I Saw It On Mulberry Street* went on to sell millions of copies and started the career of the beloved children's author, Dr. Seuss.

DURING THE AMERICAN REVOLUTION, MANY BRIDES
DID NOT WEAR WHITE GOWNS DURING THEIR WEDDING;
AS A SIGN OF REBELLION, THEY WORE RED.

COLD, HARSH CASH

A week before Christmas 1777, George Washington and his Continental Army established camp at Valley Forge, Pennsylvania, for the winter, remaining there until June 1778. It's true that as many as 2,000 men died during those six months, but it wasn't because of the weather. The close quarters were a breeding ground for typhus, typhoid, dysentery, and pneumonia, but the main killer was mismanagement and indifference. Pennsylvania farmers elected to sell their produce to the British instead of the new United States because they trusted the English sterling over the recently minted American money.

Apollos Rivoire and Deborah Hitchbourn
were French Huguenots who moved
to Boston after being driven from France.
In America, Apollos Rivoire changed
his name to Paul Rivoire, and then to
Paul Revere——the name he gave to
his first son.

I'LL DRINK TO THAT

The idea that it was against the law to drink alcoholic beverages during Prohibition [1920—1933] is patently untrue. You were free to drink as much booze as you wanted so as long as the alcohol had been purchased prior to the enactment of the Eighteenth Amendment. The National Prohibition Act, commonly referred to as the "Volstead Act," established the legal definition of intoxicating liquor as well as providing for enforcement of Prohibition. While the manufacture, sale, and transport of alcohol were illegal under Section 29 of the Volstead Act, it did allow for homemade wine and hard cider from fruit [but no beer]——up to 200 gallons per year.

DON'T FENCE ME IN

In 1626, the Dutch purchased "New Amsterdam" from the Native Americans, and soon tensions began to mount. In 1653, Dutch Governor Peter Stuyvesant ordered walls to be erected between the Hudson and East River to protect the town from marauding Indians. Originally, they were basic plank fences, but as tensions mounted, the walls became taller and stronger. In 1669, the British tore down the walls after having taken over New Amsterdam five years earlier, and they renamed it New York. The walls are gone, but they live on in the name given to the street that ran alongside them——Wall Street.

BREAKING THE RULES

John H. Eaton, U.S. senator from Tennessee, was the youngest senator ever elected. He was twenty-eight years old when he was sworn in on November 16, 1818, even though the minimum age requirement set forth in the United States Constitution is thirty years.

John Sedgwick, a Union general during
the Civil War, was killed during the Battle of
Spotsylvania Court House on May 9, 1864,
while watching Confederate troops.
His last words were, "They couldn't hit
an elephant at this distance."

IT'S THE ALABASTER PLASTER

Many of us have heard the story that the White House got its name because, after the British burned it in August 1814 during the War of 1812, it was painted white to hide the damage. And if that were true it wouldn't be in this book. Massachusetts Congressman Abijah Bigelow wrote to a colleague on March 18, 1812 [three months before the United States declared war on Britain on June 18, 1812], "There is much trouble at the White House, as we call it." The White House has been called, at various times in history, the "President's House," the "President's Palace," and the "Executive Mansion." In 1901 President Theodore Roosevelt officially named it the White House.

THEIR NATIVE TONGUE

The first Bible printed in America [the New Testament in 1661 and the full text in 1663] was not the King James version, nor was it written in English, French, or German. It was written in the Massachusetts Indian dialect——Algonquin. The "Algonquin Bible," or "Mamusse Wunneetupanatamwe up-Biblum God naneeswe Nukkone Testament kah wonk Wusku Testament," as it is technically known, was translated by John Eliot and published in Cambridge, Massachusetts.

In 1978, President Jimmy Carter,
the first Southerner elected to the
presidency following the Civil War,
restored U.S. citizenship to Jefferson Davis,
president of the Confederate States
of America.

EAT MY SHORTS, MAN

"**B**aghdad Betty," an Iraqi government propaganda broadcaster, warned American soldiers during the first Gulf War that "Bart Simpson is making love to your wife." The story, which ran rampant during the early 1990s, was supposed to be the modern equivalent of the infamous but fictitious propagandist Tokyo Rose. According to a 1991 article in the *Toronto Star*, the rumor started as a monologue by Johnny Carson on his August 22, 1990, broadcast of *The Tonight Show*. But in the original monologue the men making love to American soldiers' wives were Tom Selleck, Tom Cruise, and Homer Simpson. The story evolved to Bart Simpson, probably because it made the Iraqis seem stupid and easy to conquer.

IT WASN'T UNTIL THE EARLY 1990S THAT WOMEN WERE
ALLOWED TO WEAR PANTS ON THE SENATE FLOOR.

MENTIONING HER UNMENTIONABLES

On August 8, 1840, a Comanche war party attacked the port town of Linnville, Texas, burning, looting, and rampaging. Most of the settlers escaped in their small boats, but Juliet Watts and her husband, Hugh, ran back to their house to save their possessions. The Comanche killed Hugh and kidnapped Juliet. Days later, as the retreating Indians were attacked and defeated by a posse at the Battle of Plum Creek, Mrs. Watts was shot in the breast with an arrow. One thing stood between the arrow and certain death for Mrs. Watts——her corset.

THE FAKE GUN JOHN DILLINGER USED TO ESCAPE FROM THE LAKE COUNTY JAIL IN CROWN POINT, INDIANA, ON MARCH 3, 1934, WAS CARVED FROM WOOD—NOT SOAP.

BACK TOO SOON?

John Scott Harrison [1804—1878] was an Ohio representative and the only man to be both the father and son of U.S. presidents. His father was William Henry Harrison [ninth president] and his son was Benjamin Harrison [twenty-third president]. His body was stolen by gravediggers and sold to the Medical College of Ohio in Cincinnati for use as a training cadaver. It was eventually recovered and re-interred.

THAT'S TOO BAAAAD

In 1918 during World War I, President Woodrow Wilson allowed sheep to graze on the White House lawn to replace the gardeners who had volunteered to serve in the armed forces. He was able to raise $52,823 for the Red Cross by shearing the sheep and selling their wool.

The initials "LBJ" didn't just stand
for Lyndon Baines Johnson. They actually
stood for every member of the Johnson
family: Lady Bird Johnson, his wife;
their daughters, Lynda Bird Johnson and
Luci Baines Johnson; and the family dog,
Little Beagle Johnson.

GOT YOU UNDER MY SPELL

Theodore Roosevelt never backed down from a fight even when his opponent was Merriam-Webster. Roosevelt was a believer in simplifying the spelling of hundreds of English words, particularly eliminating silent vowels. He ordered the U.S. Government Printing Office to change the spelling of 300 specific words in all government publications. Some of the spelling changes didn't fare so well: "kissed" became "kist," "addressed" became "addrest," "blushed" became "blusht," "crossed" became "crost," and "gypsy" became "gipsy." The "s" was exchanged for a "z" in "exorcize" and "compromize," and the "e" was kicked out of the word "whisky." When Congress came back into session they debated the issue and voted against Roosevelt and his "bully" language. One word change that eventually resurfaced was the spelling of "through" to "thru."

THE DEVIL AND
WEBSTER'S DICTIONARY

Henry Watterson, editor of the *Louisville Courier-Journal*, amused or angered over Theodore Roosevelt's tampering with the English language, wrote: "Nuthing escapes Mr. Rucevelt. No subject is tu hi fr him to takl, nor tu lo for him tu notis. He makes tretis without the consent of the Senit. He inforces such laws as meet his approval, and fales to se those that du not soot him. He now assales the English langgwidg, constitutes himself a sort of French Academy, and will reform the spelling in a way tu soot himself."

IN 1937, GERTRUDE STEIN, AN AMERICAN WRITER WHO
SPENT MOST OF HER LIFE IN FRANCE, PROPOSED THAT
ADOLF HITLER RECEIVE THE NOBEL PEACE PRIZE.

MOTHER KNOWS BEST

At age fourteen, George Washington received word from his half-brother Lawrence that the British Royal Navy was seeking a new midshipman. Washington knew a spot in His Majesty's Navy would mean a lifetime of adventure as well as a wonderful career. His mother, Mary, who ruled over George most of his life, seriously considered the plan and at one point nearly gave George her blessing. But after some soul searching, Mary decided that George should stay with her and not dedicate his life to the sea. We should all be thankful for Mary Washington's decision because had she allowed George to take that appointment in 1746, he would have been fighting on the side of the British during the American Revolution!

CASHING OUT

When Grover Cleveland was drafted into the Union Army during the Civil War, he did what any other red-blooded American would do: He paid a substitute $150 to take his place. What Cleveland did was completely legal under the terms of the Conscription Act of 1863. Yep, you could pay some poor sap a couple hundred dollars and he would go fight in your place. Cleveland decided he should stay at home and support his mother and sister while his two brothers were off fighting for the Union. His actions were made a part of his opponent's campaign during Cleveland's presidential race; but because it was legal, it had no impact on the voters.

WHAT'S THE FLAPPER
ALL ABOUT?

We've all heard glamorous stories of the Roaring Twenties, traditionally viewed as an era of great economic prosperity before the Great Crash of '29, when everyone was living high on the hog. But like many generalizations, it doesn't hold up under scrutiny. In fact, according to the Brookings Institution, although a handful of people did make fortunes, most people didn't get the lion's share of the Roaring Twenties. In 1929, 60 percent of American families had annual incomes of $2,000 or less [and 42 percent of these had annual incomes of less than $1,500]. In 1929, families making less than $2,000 did not have enough money to meet the bare necessities of life——meaning nearly two-thirds of the population lived in poverty.

STRETCHING THE TRUTH

Although lynching was popularized during the Old West, the practice actually started during the American Revolution. Colonel Charles Lynch, a justice of the peace and farmer before the war, led a group of vigilantes to dispense swift and final justice on British supporters and outlaws. Soon, stringing someone up without a trial became known as "lynching," and the groups that performed the activity were called "lynch mobs."

On Christmas Day in 1868, President Andrew Johnson's last significant act was granting unconditional amnesty to all Confederate soldiers for their actions in the Civil War. Confederate President Jefferson Davis declined to accept it.

HIS FINAL BOW

As one of his last official acts as president, Bill Clinton took it upon himself to take care of the number six man on the Department of Justice's list of "Most Wanted" international fugitives, Marc Rich. He gave him a full presidential pardon. But Rich wasn't the only beneficiary of Clinton's exit strategy: Carlos Anibal Vignali, who was serving fifteen years in prison for organized cocaine trafficking, got his prison sentence commuted, as did Almon Glenn Braswell, who had been convicted of mail fraud and perjury. In all, Clinton pardoned 140 people in the final days of his administration.

Hugh Rodham, brother of Hillary Rodham Clinton, lobbied the president for some of these pardons, receiving $400,000 in compensation. When ethical questions were raised [surprise], Rodham returned the money.

WHAT DID YOU CALL ME?

The Pilgrims who sailed on the *Mayflower* never referred to themselves as "Pilgrims." More than likely, they called themselves "Separatists" or even "Saints." The name "Pilgrim" was bestowed on them after the fact and was taken from William Bradford's journal [written between 1620 and 1647], *Of Plimoth Plantation* [in contemporary spelling, *Of Plymouth Plantation*]. Bradford gave this name to his fellow travelers because a "pilgrim" is someone who takes a pilgrimage or an extensive journey to a holy location. Even though less than half of the 102 passengers on board the *Mayflower* were on a religious pilgrimage, Bradford referred to everyone on the voyage as pilgrims.

IN 1643, THE COLONY OF NEW PLYMOUTH, MASSACHUSETTS, IMPOSED THE FIRST RECORDED INCOME TAX IN AMERICA.

A FLAGGING INTEREST

In paintings, movies, and on television, we're given the impression that worshipping the flag was something all devout Americans have done since the War of Independence, but that's not exactly the way it was. Schools were not required to fly the flag until 1890. Pledging allegiance to the flag wasn't instituted until 1892, and saluting the flag didn't happen until the time of the Spanish-American War in 1898. It wasn't until 1916 that Flag Day was observed as a national holiday, and the flag code, the proper way to treat and dispose of flags, was not approved by Congress until 1942 and didn't become a federal law until 1976.

AND SEE WHO SALUTES IT

So if Betsy Ross didn't design the first flag, who did? That person was probably Francis Hopkinson. On May 25, 1780, he wrote a letter to the Continental Board of Admiralty requesting a reward of "a Quarter Cask of the public Wine" for several patriotic designs he had created during the previous three years, including "the Flag of the United States of America." The request was sent to the Treasury Board, which turned it down in an October 27, 1780, report to Congress. The Board based their decision on the fact that Hopkinson "was not the only person consulted on those exhibitions of Fancy, and therefore cannot claim the sole merit of them and not entitled to the full sum charged."

FLAG RUNNER UP

We know Betsy Ross was a poor, recently widowed, struggling seamstress who was secretly approached by General George Washington and two others, at a clandestine nighttime meeting. They begged for her help in creating the flag. So who is this Francis Hopkinson fellow trying to steal all the glory for creating Old Glory? Hopkinson was an American author, and, as a delegate from New Jersey, he was one of the signers of the Declaration of Independence.

IN THE WRONG KEY

Some mistakenly believe that Francis Scott Key was an avid supporter of the War of 1812 and a known patriot——he was neither. Key was on board the British ship *HMS Tonnant* accompanied by American prisoner exchange agent Colonel John Stuart Skinner to negotiate the freeing of a political prisoner. In fact, Key was against the War of 1812, condemning "this abominable war" as a "lump of wickedness," and writing his mother that he thought the United States was the aggressor in the conflict and deserved defeat.

IN 1861, FRANCIS SCOTT KEY'S GRANDSON WAS IMPRISONED
IN FORT MCHENRY (WHERE FRANCIS SAW THAT "THE FLAG
WAS STILL THERE") ALONG WITH THE MAYOR OF BALTIMORE
AND OTHER LOCALS DEEMED TO BE PRO-SOUTH.

THE ODD COUPLE

It's a romantic image to think of two of our founding fathers and best friends, Thomas Jefferson and John Adams, both dying on the Fourth of July in 1826 [exactly fifty years after the adoption of the Declaration of Independence]. Each was thinking of the other just before he died. Adams is even supposed to have remarked just before he passed away, "Jefferson still survives." But were they friends? Well, just five years before their deaths, Adams accused Jefferson of plagiarizing the Declaration of Independence from the Mecklenburg Declaration, a document of North Carolina independence, which supposedly dated back to 1775. "Mr. Jefferson," Adams wrote a friend, "must have seen it, in the time of it, for he has copied the spirit, the sense, and the expressions of it verbatim, into his Declaration of the 4th of July, 1776." The authenticity of the Mecklenburg Declaration of Independence is still in question.

RAISE YOUR HAND
IF YOU'RE NOT SURE

Between 1892 and 1942, Americans were taught to salute the flag with the so-called Bellamy salute [named after Francis Bellamy, 1855—1931, to accompany the Pledge of Allegiance, which he had written]: The "right hand [is] lifted, palm downward, to a line with the forehead and close to it." But when the Nazis came into power, their salute and the American salute looked a little too similar for comfort. So, by order of Congress in 1942, Americans began "saluting" the flag by putting their right hand over their hearts.

"I pledge allegiance to the Flag of the United States of America and to the Republic for which it stands; one Nation, indivisible, with liberty and justice for all." President Dwight Eisenhower signed a bill into law on Flag Day [June 14, 1954] that added the words "under God" after "one Nation."

TA-DA!

To commemorate the death of master magician Harry Houdini, Joseph W. "Amazing Joe" Burrus tried to better one of Houdini's famous stunts on October 31, 1990. Burrus was chained and locked, placed in a clear plastic coffin of his own making, and lowered into the ground. Then dirt and finally seven tons of concrete were poured on top of the coffin. Before Burrus could escape, the weight of the concrete crushed the coffin, and he died exactly sixty-four Halloweens from the day the Great Houdini died. J. D. Bristow, the stuntman's assistant on the fatal night, said Burrus made no attempt to calculate the weight of the dirt and concrete and tested the strength of the plastic coffin simply by jumping on it.

WHEN THE CIVIL WAR STARTED, UNION GENERAL
ULYSSES S. GRANT OWNED SLAVES, BUT CONFEDERATE
GENERAL ROBERT E. LEE DID NOT.

A House Divided

Fighting in the Civil War wasn't all about glory, romanticism, unifying the country, or even freeing the slaves——it was also about money. More than 100,000 soldiers, mostly immigrants, were hired to fight for the North. However, if you were already rich and didn't need the money, or you didn't want to fight in the war, you could legally get out of the conscription by paying a $300 commutation fee. Some well-known people who paid their way out were banker J. P. Morgan and Theodore Roosevelt, Sr., father of President Theodore Roosevelt. But if paying wasn't an option, then you could do what more than 200,000 Union soldiers did after the war started——they deserted.

A FAREWELL TO ARMS

Ernest Hemingway has always been portrayed as a brave, hard-drinking, hard-living hunter, soldier, and writer——but he wasn't all those things. Hemingway did serve in World War I, but not as a soldier. He was a volunteer with the American Red Cross. He was wounded by mortar fire, but while serving chocolates to the soldiers. He was also in both the Spanish Civil War and World War II, but he served only as a reporter. Apparently, Hemingway's ability to weave a great story wasn't confined to the written page; he falsely claimed he was the first American wounded in Italy [after carrying an Italian soldier on his back to safety]. He was never, as he claimed, wounded by machine-gun fire; he didn't join the Sixty-Ninth Infantry; and he never fought in three major Italian battles.

HORATIO NO YOU DIDN'T

The rags-to-riches stories of American author Horatio Alger are considered by many critics to be overly romantic and poorly written. Alger fans didn't care, because they bought his books by the millions, making him one of the best-selling authors of all times. But the chief complaint about Alger had nothing to do with his literary aptitude, but more with his morality. Alger, it turned out, was a notorious pedophile. According to Unitarian church records, in 1866, when Alger was a young pastor in Brewster, Massachusetts, several boys in his congregation accused him of using his position to take advantage of them sexually. Before he could be punished for his crimes, Alger left town and ended up in New York City, where he became known as a writer of children's fiction.

JUST SQUEAKING BY

D id Mickey Mouse make his debut in the animated short *Steamboat Willie*? Well, if he did, he wouldn't be in this book. Actually, Mickey first appeared in a silent film called *Plane Crazy*, but it was *Steamboat Willie* that was first shown in public. The movie made its debut at the Colony Theater in New York on November 18, 1928, and was the first cartoon that successfully incorporated synchronized sound. That is why November 18 is officially considered Mickey's birthday. But what do you get for a mouse that has everything?

WE DESERVE A BREAK TODAY

We've all heard the name Ray Kroc before——he's the guy who founded McDonald's. But if he was the founder, why didn't he call his franchise Kroc's, or even McKroc's? Obviously, no one would eat at a restaurant named McKroc's, but the real reason is that he wasn't the restaurant's founder. Richard and Maurice McDonald opened their first drive-in restaurant near Pasadena, California, and they started McDonald's in 1940. In 1954, Ray Kroc, who was a milkshake-machine salesman, bought the franchise rights from the brothers and eventually acquired the McDonald's name for $14 million. He completed his buyout in 1961. So, saying that Ray Kroc founded McDonald's is, well, a bunch of crock.

WOODROW WILSON WAS THE ONLY PRESIDENT WITH A PHD. HE EARNED IT FROM JOHNS HOPKINS UNIVERSITY IN 1886.

WHAT'S BUGGIN' YA?

In 1947, the U.S. Navy's Mark II computer at Harvard University crashed after a moth got jammed in a relay switch. The operators removed the fried flutter-by and taped it in their logbook alongside the explanation of the occurrence. It's a true story, but it doesn't describe the origin of the term "bug" [as in "computer bug"]. A newspaper report from 1889, cited in the *Oxford English Dictionary*, related that Thomas Edison "had been up the two previous nights searching for a bug in his phonograph." And the 1934 edition of Webster's dictionary also gave the definition of bug as it related to a screw-up in a mechanical or electrical device.

EGG ON HIS FACE

In case you've ever wondered, Eggs Benedict is not named for the famous traitor Benedict Arnold. The origin of the name for the breakfast dish that consists of a half of an English muffin topped with ham or bacon, poached eggs, and hollandaise sauce is a mystery. Lemuel Benedict claimed he concocted the dish in 1894 at the Waldorf Hotel as a hangover remedy. Or maybe it was Commodore E. C. Benedict, or Mrs. Le Grand Benedict, or even the explanation given in the book *French Provincial Cooking*, which describes a traditional French dish named *œufs bénédictine*. However the name came about, it definitely has nothing to do with Benedict Arnold because if it was it would more than likely have been called Eggs Arnold.

AMENDING THE AMENDMENTS

There's only been one time in our nation's history when one amendment to the Constitution was enacted to cancel out an earlier amendment. That took place in 1933 when the Twenty-First Amendment repealed the Eighteenth Amendment, which had prohibited the manufacture, sale, and transportation of liquor in the United States in 1919——basically, the Twenty-First Amendment prohibited Prohibition.

W hile a high school student in the
early 1930s, Richard Nixon worked for
two summers as a barker for the
wheel-of-chance at the Slippery Gulch
Rodeo in Prescott, Arizona.

GET THIS PARTY STARTED

The Republican party likes to refer to itself as the GOP or the Grand Old Party. But that isn't what GOP always stood for. The initials date back to the 1870s when they stood for "this gallant old party" in the 1875 Congressional Record. There is another reference in 1876 to "Grand Old Party," and "Get Out and Push" was used as a party slogan in the 1920s. But whether it's gallant or grand, it isn't the oldest party. The Democrat party organized in 1830 under Andrew Jackson actually is an off-shoot of the Democratic-Republicans from the era of Thomas Jefferson.

NEVER MORE

We all have the image of a stumbling Edgar Allan Poe, stoned out of his mind, passing out on a Baltimore sidewalk shortly before he died. We all know he was macabre, morbid, an alcoholic, and a dope fiend but still one of the greatest writers in American literature and the creator of the detective story. But most of the horrible attributes aren't true. An envious writer named Rufus Griswold, who wrote a biographical article of Poe called "Memoir of the Author," created them. Griswold wrote that Poe had "criminal relations with his Mother in Law," was a drunkard who was kicked out of both the University of Virginia and West Point, and was a depraved, drug-addled madman. Griswold used forged letters supposedly written by Poe to prove his case, and it was from this article that most people have garnered their information.

IF YOU LICK IT, IT'S A QUARTER

The United States Post Office printed a new 60-cent stamp in 1999 that commemorated the Grand Canyon. It was a large, beautiful stamp that showed the canyon and bore the words "Grand Canyon, Colorado." The only problem is the Grand Canyon is in Arizona. Officials decided to destroy all 100 million stamps they had produced at a cost of about $500,000, and they reprinted the stamps with correct wording. The new and improved stamp went on sale in January 2000, but it was soon pointed out that the picture of the Grand Canyon was reversed, creating a mirror image of the canyon. The U.S.P.O. decided that since the stamps were already on sale, they would stick with the new stamp anyway.

BULLY OR JUST PLAIN BULL?

The image of hundreds of men on horseback led by a barrel-chested Teddy Roosevelt, sword in hand, yelling "charge" as they conquered San Juan Hill and turned the tide of the Spanish-American War in favor of the Americans is an enduring image. It was that image that Teddy Roosevelt used in his charge into the White House, but it didn't happen. The "Rough Riders" charged Kettle Hill, not San Juan Hill, on foot because there wasn't enough room on board the ships for the men, their supplies, and their horses. So even though Roosevelt was famous for saying "bully"——he also said a lot of bull#$&t.

Colonel Leonard Wood, not Roosevelt,
was actually in command of the charge
on Kettle Hill. After the battle the
"Rough Riders" renamed themselves
"Wood's Weary Walkers."

WHAT'S IN A NAME?

Ulysses Simpson Grant was born in 1822 to Jesse and Hanna Grant. Actually, Jesse and Hanna Grant did have a baby boy but, when they finally named him a month later, they called him Hiram Ulysses Grant: Hiram for his grandfather and Ulysses for the Greek hero. When Hiram joined the U.S. Military Academy, his congressman incorrectly listed him as Ulysses Simpson Grant. Grant, who always disliked his name because his initials spelled H.U.G., decided to keep his newly appointed name. He never adopted it formally but used it as his own for the rest of his life.

THE SLAVERY BILL

A lot of revisionists [people who want to rewrite history to make it politically correct] have torn into President Thomas Jefferson because he owned slaves. Some have even gone so far as to suggest removing his picture from the $2 bill [yes, there is a $2 bill]. But if we're going to be consistent, we're going to be short a lot of money. There have been nine other presidents who also owned slaves: Washington [on the quarter and the $1 bill], Andrew Jackson [$20 bill], and Ulysses S. Grant [$50 bill]. The other presidents——James Madison, James Monroe, John Tyler, James Knox Polk, Zachary Taylor, and Andrew Johnson—— owned slaves, but they aren't on U.S. currency.

THE PRESIDENTIAL LOOK

When Gerald Ford was chosen by Nixon to replace Spiro Agnew, many people wondered, "Who is this guy? What's he done before?" Well, among other things as a young man, Gerald Ford appeared in a 1939 edition of *Look* magazine with his girlfriend Phyllis Brown. It was an article about a weekend in the life of the "beautiful people." He later appeared on the cover of *Cosmopolitan*. Seems to make him as qualified to be president as nearly anyone else.

GRIN AND BEAR IT

At the Battle of Vicksburg during the Civil War, a servant girl accidentally poured out a basin containing Ulysses S. Grant's false teeth into the Mississippi River. He was unable to eat solid food for a week until a dentist came and made him a new set of choppers.

Julia Ward Howe [1819—1910] sold
her poem, *Battle Hymn of the Republic*,
which later was set to music, to the
Atlantic Monthly in 1862 for $5.

BRAND NAMES

Most people are stuck with the name they are given at birth unless they legally change it. However, in the history of the United States, there have been five presidents who altered their name——just a little. Grover Cleveland's real name was Stephen Grover Cleveland [which has a nice ring to it], but he decided to drop his first name, as did Thomas Woodrow Wilson and John Calvin Coolidge. Dwight David Eisenhower's real name was David Dwight Eisenhower; he didn't like the order and reversed his first and middle name.

There are four presidents who
are known by their initials:
Franklin Delano Roosevelt [FDR], John
Fitzgerald Kennedy [JFK], Lyndon Baines
Johnson [LBJ], and Theodore Roosevelt,
who hated the nickname "Teddy" and
preferred "TR" instead.

JOHNNY REBEL

John Tyler wasn't honored after his death on January 18, 1862, and no official word of his death was ever issued. Why? Because Tyler was considered a traitor in the North even though he had been president of the United States. On May 5, 1861, Tyler accepted a seat in the provisional congress of the Confederate States of America. A few months later, he was elected to represent his congressional district in the permanent C.S.A. Congress. Tyler was truly a rebel and the only president to ever hold office in the Confederacy. When he died, he even had the Confederate flag, not the American flag, draped over his casket. It wasn't until 1915, fifty years after the Civil War ended, that the United States finally erected a memorial stone over his grave.

THE GOOD OLE DAYS— PART II

Here are more verbatim excerpts from the *Historical Summary of Conduct Cases in the House of Representatives* by the Committee on Standards of Official Conduct. Makes modern congressmen seem like pussycats.

★ Representative William J. Graves [KY] and Representative Henry Wise [VA], Breach of the privileges of the House Representative Graves killed Representative Jonathan Cilley [ME] in a duel over words spoken in debate; Representative Wise acted as a second [Feb. 24, 1838].

★ Representative Philemon Herbert [CA], [1856] Arrested for manslaughter [May 8, 1856]; imprisoned prior to trial; acquitted [July 1856].

★ Representative Lovell H. Rousseau [KY] [1866] Assaulted Representative Josiah Grinnell [IA] with a cane outside the Capitol for alleged insult spoken in debate [June 14, 1866].

BUT DO YOU HAVE A
RECORD OF IT?

Thomas Edison worked on the ground floor of a telegraph company that used to be a restaurant and was literally crawling with cockroaches. The roaches, he said, would crawl out of the walls and up on his table while he was writing telegraphs. So he used his inventive mind and created a roach zapper. He placed a piece of tin foil on the ground and hooked it up to a "big battery supply current to the wires," so when the cockroach scampered across it "there was a flash of light and the cockroach went into gas."

KEEP YOUR TRAP SHUT

Ralph Waldo Emerson was an American essayist, philosopher, and poet who is continuously quoted as saying that if you build a better mousetrap "The world will beat a path to your door." The genesis of that idea is contained in a journal entry written in 1855: "If a man can make better chairs or knives, crucibles or church organs, than anybody else, you will find a broad hard-beaten road to his house . . ." But nothing about mousetraps. Scholars have scoured Emerson's writings and have concluded that he never wrote anything about mousetraps. Apparently, Sarah Yule and Mary Keene, in a book published in 1889 [seven years after Emerson's death], decided that the list of things for which a man can earn public attention wouldn't be complete without a mousetrap, so they just threw that one in.

BUT WHO'S COUNTING?

When the Nineteenth Amendment to the Constitution was ratified on August 18, 1920, women were finally given the right to vote. Sounds pretty cut and dry, but of course, history is anything but cut and dry. During various times throughout American history, some women already had the right to vote, such as in local elections during colonial times in Massachusetts, New York, New Jersey, Rhode Island, and Pennsylvania. And between 1776 and 1807, women who were worth at least 50 pounds had the right to vote in New Jersey. In 1869, the Territory of Wyoming granted women voting rights in all elections, the Territory of Utah followed in 1870, and in 1883, so did the Territory of Washington. By the time the Nineteenth Amendment was ratified, women already had the vote in fifteen of the forty-eight states.

WHILE MARTIN VAN BUREN WAS VICE PRESIDENT UNDER
ANDREW JACKSON, HE ROUTINELY PRESIDED OVER THE
SENATE WEARING A PAIR OF LOADED PISTOLS.

RUN OUT ON A RAIL

Abraham Lincoln's life is so steeped in myth, fiction, and legend that it's difficult to know what to believe. Like this oft-quoted pro-tariff statement attributed to him: "I do not know much about the tariff, but I know this much, when we buy manufactured goods abroad, we get the goods and the manufacturer gets the money. When we buy manufactured goods at home, we get both the goods and the money. When an American paid $20 for steel rails to an English manufacturer, America had the steel and England the $20. But when he paid $20 for the steel to an American manufacturer, America had both the steel and the $20." This one is easy to disprove. The reason Lincoln couldn't have said it was that he died before the first steel rails were brought into, or manufactured in, the United States.

DIFFERENT SIDES
OF THE SAME COIN

It is widely believed that most colonists wanted freedom from the tyranny of Great Britain and that there were few "loyalists," or people who remained loyal to the crown. That's simply not the case. In fact, there were a great number of loyalists who fought against the patriots. For example, in 1780 there were 9,000 patriots in Washington's army while 8,000 loyalists served in the British Army.

ALWAYS ON THE WINNING SIDE

What is now Jackson, New Hampshire, was originally known as New Madbury, New Hampshire. The town changed its name in 1800 to Adams to honor the election of President John Adams. But in 1829, when John Adams's son John Quincy Adams lost the election to Andrew Jackson, the town changed its name to Jackson, New Hampshire.

IN NOVEMBER 1939 DURING THE GREAT DEPRESSION,
FRANKLIN D. ROOSEVELT ORDERED THAT THANKSGIVING BE
CELEBRATED ONE WEEK EARLIER THAN USUAL, THEREBY
EXTENDING THE CHRISTMAS SHOPPING SEASON.

KEEPING UP WITH THE JONESES

Revolutionary hero John Paul Jones was actually born John Paul in 1747. He added the Jones part later. He is remembered for his bravery on the high seas and for supposedly remarking, "I've just begun to fight." But what isn't remembered about Jones is what he did after the Revolution. He left the United States, and in 1788 he became a well-paid mercenary in the service of Empress Catherine II of Russia. Once in her service, Jones once again took liberty with his name and changed from John Paul Jones to Pavel Dzhones.

A Jury of Your Peers

One would think that after women were given the right to vote in 1920, everything would be equal among the sexes. Far from it. As late as 1942, women only had the right to sit on a jury in twenty-eight states. It wasn't until 1957 that they were guaranteed the right to sit on federal juries. In 1973 they were finally given the right to sit on all juries in all fifty states.

When Jimmy Carter was the thirty-ninth
president of the United States, he kissed
England's queen mother, Queen Elizabeth,
on the lips. It was a shocking breach
of etiquette that even obituary writers
noted upon her death.

BOSTON BEANS

If there's one thing that makes Americans stiffen with pride and justification, it's the Boston Massacre. The idea of a group of fierce, armed British soldiers firing into a quivering, innocent group of patriots is beyond belief. And it should be, because it didn't happen the way we're led to believe. You see, it was the Americans who started the fight. The colonists were reacting to an incident earlier in the day. To protest the British presence in their town, a large angry mob estimated at between 300 and 400 people surrounded a small British garrison and threatened the troops with clubs and rocks. After Private Hugh Montgomery was struck with a club, he fired his weapon and other British soldiers followed suit. Five colonists were killed [three at the scene and two died later from their wounds], and six others were hurt.

B4 BOSTON

There were several less propagandized run-ins with the British before the Boston Massacre. A patriot in New York was wounded with a bayonet during a skirmish with British troops in 1766. Two years later, a Rhode Island man was killed in an argument with a British naval officer. And in New York in January 1770, there was a nasty battle between redcoats and patriots. The following month, during a patriot attack on the home of a Boston Tory, an eleven-year-old boy was killed.

HELL OF A PARTY

Another great event in the history of the United States is the infamous Boston Tea Party. You know the story. On December 16, 1773, a group of colonists, angry at paying higher taxes on their tea, dressed up like Indians and dumped crates of tea bricks belonging to the British East India Company into the Boston Harbor. Not sure why we're so proud of an act of vandalism, but that's beside the point. The point is, the Tea Act, which the colonists were supposedly angry about, actually reduced the duty on British tea imported to America. So why did they really revolt? Because once British tea was affordable, it would ruin America's lucrative trade in black-market tea, because three-fourths of the tea sold in America was smuggled in by John Hancock. Now the whole idea of dressing up like Indians makes sense, doesn't it?

I Got No Strings
to Hold Me Down

Richard Nixon resigned his presidency after it was uncovered that he had ordered the break-in of the Democratic election headquarters at the Watergate apartment complex in Washington, D.C. Years later, John Barrett, the first undercover officer to arrive on the scene, finally explained how the burglars had been apprehended. Apparently, the lookout stationed in the Howard Johnson Motel across the street did not see Barrett arrive because he was busy watching a movie on TV. The movie in question was the 1958 thriller *Attack of the Puppet People*.

The Watergate burglars used tape to hold down a door's spring-loaded lock mechanism so as not to be locked in. Their trick was noticed, however, because they applied the tape horizontally around the door rather than vertically along its edge.

AND I'LL CRY IF I WANT TO

Although used as a catalyst to initiate the war for independence, not everyone agreed with the actions perpetrated during the Boston Tea Party. In fact, Benjamin Franklin suggested the colonists should reimburse the East India Company for the destroyed tea. A New York merchant, Robert Murray, and three others visited Lord North and offered to pay for the losses, but the offer was turned down.

A REAL STICKY SITUATION

On an unusually warm January day in 1919, the fifty-foot-high tank at the Purity Distilling Company in Boston, Massachusetts, which contained more than 2 million gallons of steam-heated molasses, burst, sending a tidal wave of molasses into the streets. The wave, which reached fifteen feet, traveled at thirty-five miles an hour; it crushed trolley cars, swallowed trucks, horses, and carts, knocked buildings off their foundations, killed twenty-one people, and wounded 150 others. Finally, the molasses began to cool and congeal, and rescue teams arrived to help the survivors and find the victims. When the Red Cross workers arrived, they helped bandage the wounded and gave the survivors fresh hot coffee——sweetened with the molasses that still ran in the streets.

FORGING ANOTHER MYTH

Freezing, half-naked, half-starved soldiers leaving bloody footprints in the snow or shivering, huddled over a small fire——that's what most of us think of when we hear about Valley Forge during the winter of 1777—1778. But studies by the National Park Service showed that nobody starved or froze to death, and morale was high. The men usually had plenty to eat as the camp was supplied each month with a million pounds of flour and a million pounds of meat and fish. The men didn't live in the open but had constructed log houses that they described as "cozy and comfortable quarters." Not to say that there wasn't suffering or disease, but it wasn't the horrible situation we've been led to believe. And who led us to believe this way? General George Washington himself. Wanting to make sure his men had the supplies they needed, he resorted to stretching the truth a little about their situation.

The belief that some of the men went "naked" at Valley Forge results from misunderstanding the eighteenth-century use of the word. The term "naked" implied that the men did not wear proper clothing and were therefore considered unfit for duty, not that they had no clothes at all.

THE CANE MUTINY

Charles Sumner, the Massachusetts senator who was clubbed over the head with a cane by a South Carolina representative, has become part of Civil War mythology. The event did happen, and it did follow Sumner's passionate speech on the "barbarism of slavery." But was the attack so severe that it left Sumner virtually incapacitated for three years? According to David Donald's Pulitzer prize—winning biography of Sumner, there is nothing in the senator's medical record to explain why he couldn't execute his duties. It's assumed that Sumner suffered more psychological than physical harm from the attack.

"ELEVATE THEM GUNS A LITTLE LOWER!"

——*President Andrew Jackson, in 1815, at the battle of Mobile, Alabama*

AFFORD THE TRUTH

Henry Ford popularized both the automobile and the assembly line, but he was in no way responsible for their invention. The first automobile [non-gasoline powered] was the Puffing Devil, built and demonstrated by Richard Trevithick in 1801. Some suggest that Nicolas-Joseph Cugnot preceded Trevithick by more than thirty years, or even that Ferdinand Verbiest should be given credit for his steam-powered car built in 1672. However, there's no conclusive proof that either of these machines actually worked. The belief that Ford invented the moving assembly line is also an unwarranted claim. Ransom Olds [of Oldsmobile fame] patented the assembly line concept in 1901, and Ford implemented his assembly line in 1913.

SPIRITS OF AMERICA

After retiring from the presidency on March 4, 1797, George Washington returned home to Mount Vernon and started a new career as a producer of whiskey. He constructed a 2,250 square foot distillery that housed five copper stills, a boiler, and fifty mash tubs. It became one of the largest distilleries in America at the time. Two years after its construction, the distillery produced 11,000 gallons of corn and rye whiskey and fruit brandy.

A NOTE TO CONGRESS

Thomas Jefferson only communicated with Congress through written messages, even though his predecessors addressed the legislature in person. Because of this practice, it wasn't until Woodrow Wilson that presidents began appearing in front of Congress personally. It is rumored that Jefferson wrote as opposed to speaking because he was a poor orator but an excellent writer.

If you think members of Congress
are sneaky now [which you should because
they are], look at the forty-second Congress
of 1873. It not only gave itself a salary
raise of 50 percent, but then made it
retroactive for two years.

HOME SICK

It's a type of rags to riches story, but it's more along the lines of a sick to healthy story. Theodore Roosevelt said that as a child, he was very sick and chronically asthmatic, but with fresh air and exercise, he became known as one of the most physically active presidents in history. However, in his biography of Roosevelt, David McCullough states that even though Roosevelt may have suffered as a child, he might not have been as sick as we've been led to believe. It seems that his asthma attacks occurred only on Sundays——the one day of the week that his father was at home.

PULIT SURPRISE

John F. Kennedy is the only president to date who has won the Pulitzer Prize. He was honored with the prestigious award in 1957 for his book *Profiles in Courage*. But like a lot of myths surrounding "Camelot," this one isn't quite true. Kennedy did win the Prize, but did he really write the book by himself? No. One of his speechwriters, Theodore Sorensen, actually penned most the book. This fact has been rumored for years, but it was Sorensen's own autobiography in 2008 that let the cat out of the bag. Sorensen wrote that he "did a first draft of most chapters," "helped choose the words of many of its sentences," and "privately boasted or indirectly hinted that [he] had written much of the book."

WHAT'S IN A DREAM

It's a chilling story and another fascinating aspect of the life of President Abraham Lincoln——that he had a premonition of his own death by an assassin's bullet. Several days before his death, Lincoln told of a dream in which he had been awakened in the White House by mournful cries and discovered that the wailing voices were coming from the East Room. "There I met with a sickening surprise. Before me was a catafalque, on which rested a corpse wrapped in funeral vestments. 'Who is dead in the White House?' I demanded of one of the soldiers. 'The President' was his answer; 'he was killed by an assassin.'" So Lincoln *did* predict his own death! No, because when the story was originally published, Lincoln made it clear that it wasn't he who had been killed. "In this dream," the president was quoted as saying, "it was not me, but some other fellow, that was killed. It seems that this ghostly assassin tried his hand on someone else."

NOT VERY REVERED

In July 1779, forty-five American ships sailed into Penobscot Bay where the British held a half-finished fort, but the Americans did nothing to provoke the enemy. Even though they outnumbered the British, they waited for weeks without taking any action, and that gave the British plenty of time to bring in reinforcements. Confronted by a well-manned army and navy, the American ships fled up the Penobscot River. Realizing they might be attacked by the British and have their supplies and ships captured, they decided to burn seventeen of their own ships and fled by foot. Paul Revere [yes, that Paul Revere], who was the commander of artillery, was charged by the Continental Army with cowardice and insubordination. [One military committee ruled that Revere's conduct was "crityzable"; another that it was not.] However, Revere was acquitted during his court martial in 1782.

ANY LAST WORDS?

An interesting story about Benedict Arnold, and one that shows he repented his treason, is that on his death bed he cried out, "Let me die in my American uniform in which I fought my battles. God forgive me for ever putting on any other." It's a great redemptive story, but it isn't true. After his death, Arnold's wife Margaret "Peggy" Shippen Arnold wrote that Benedict had been delirious in his last three days and wasn't able to swallow or speak a word.

WHEN JOHN F. KENNEDY WAS ASSASSINATED IN
DALLAS IN 1963, IT WAS NOT A FEDERAL FELONY TO KILL
A PRESIDENT OF THE UNITED STATES.

THE FINAL ACT

Pulitzer Prize— and Tony Award—winning playwright Tennessee Williams, famous for *A Streetcar Named Desire* and *Cat on a Hot Tin Roof,* suffocated to death at the age of seventy-one on February 24, 1983, in his room at the Hotel Elysee in New York City. Coroners discovered that Williams had choked to death on an eye-drop bottle cap, which friends said he would routinely place in his mouth when he tilted back his head to administer the eye drops.

The Woodstock Festival, technically called The Woodstock Music and Art Fair, was actually held at Max Yasgur's dairy farm in the rural town of Bethel, New York, forty-three miles southwest of Woodstock, New York.

ENGLISH FIRST

Martin Van Buren, the first president born an American citizen [his predecessors were born before the War of Independence] grew up speaking Dutch, which made him the only president not to have spoken English as a first language [unless, of course, you include George W. Bush].

In 1872, Congress passed a law requiring members of both houses to be docked a day's pay for every day's absence, except in the case of illness. More than 135 years later, the law has been enforced only twice.

THE SHOT HEARD
AROUND THE WORLD

In a horrible perversion on the old saying, "third time's a charm," John Wilkes Booth was actually the third assassin who attempted to take the life of President Abraham Lincoln. Lincoln had been the target of two failed assassination attempts, both times while on his way to his cottage at the Soldiers' Home on the outskirts of Washington, D.C. In his book *Abraham Lincoln*, Carl Sandburg tells of the first attempt in 1861, when Lincoln was shot at by a man standing less than fifty yards away. Then in August 1864, he was shot at again, and this time the bullet passed through the upper part of his famous stovepipe hat. But it was that third, fatal bullet we all remember, fired at pointblank range on April 14, 1865.

WHAT'S BURNIN' YA?

The War of 1812 is remembered [if at all] for one thing——the burning of the White House by those dastardly British. Invading a country is one thing, but to maliciously burn down important and cherished buildings is just mean. But that's just what *we* did to the British before they did it to us. The Americans attacked York, the capital of Upper Canada [which became Toronto, Ontario], on April 27, 1813, and burned dozens of buildings including the Parliament, all without orders. Because of this malicious attack, the British retaliated with their burning of Washington, D.C. on August 24, 1814.

TAKE A LETTER

O n November 21, 1864, the *Boston Evening Transcript* printed a letter from President Abraham Lincoln to Mrs. Lydia Bixby, a widow who was "the mother of five sons who have died gloriously on the field of battle." The letter, known as the Bixby Letter, was both heartfelt and beautifully written, but there are two things wrong with it. One, it probably wasn't written by Abraham Lincoln [Lincoln's secretary John Hay later claimed to have penned the letter], and two, Mrs. Bixby's sons weren't all killed. According to War Department statistics, only two of Bixby's sons died [Charles and Oliver], one deserted, another was honorably discharged, and one was captured and became a Confederate [or died a POW]. The original letter doesn't exist as Mrs. Bixby, who was a Confederate sympathizer and disliked President Lincoln, destroyed it shortly after it was delivered.

SOLDIERS OF MISFORTUNE

It was the most notorious military prison during the Civil War——
Camp Sumter, commonly referred to as Andersonville Prison,
located in Andersonville, Georgia. Of the 45,000 Union prisoners held
there 12,913 died of malnutrition and disease——approximately 100
prisoners died every day. But it wasn't out of cruelty that the soldiers
suffered so during their imprisonment, it was primarily because of
overcrowding and the fact that the South couldn't afford to feed,
clothe, or provide proper medical treatment for the prisoners. Other
military prisons didn't fare much better. In fact, of the 195,000 Union
soldiers imprisoned in the South, 15.5 percent died; and of the 215,000
Confederates imprisoned in the North, 12 percent died.

The commandant at Camp Sumter, Henry Wirz, was court-martialed, found guilty of war crimes, and hanged on November 10, 1865. Wirz was the only Confederate official to be tried and convicted of war crimes resulting from the Civil War.

SHORT AND STOUT

As ten-year-old Henry Ford watched steam rising from his mother's teapot, he deduced that if the steam were confined, it could raise the teapot into the air. He took a clay teapot, filled it with water, corked the spout, tied down the lid and placed the teapot in the fireplace. He watched the teapot carefully for signs that it was about to lift off, but what it did was blast off, or actually, blast apart. The exploding teapot broke a window and a mirror, scalded and cut young Henry, and left a scar on his face that he carried with him for the rest of his life.

DURING THE 1918 INFLUENZA PANDEMIC, THE DEATH TOLL IN THE UNITED STATES WAS SO HIGH THERE WAS A SHORTAGE OF COFFINS.

DUDE LOOKS LIKE A LADY

A story told by Civil War buffs about Confederate president Jefferson Davis was that he had disguised himself in his wife's clothing when he was arrested on May 10, 1865. The event was widely publicized, and articles and cartoons portrayed Jefferson as a humiliated, cross-dressing coward. But, like many Civil War myths, it's not true. "I was in the party that captured Davis," Captain James H. Parker wrote later. "Jefferson Davis did not have on, at the time he was taken, any garments such as are worn by women."

LOOSE LIPS

The unprovoked sinking of the *Lusitania* is regarded by many as the inciting incident that brought the United States into World War I. Although the sinking incident did heighten anti-German sentiment, it didn't bring the Americans into the war. Here are the facts: First, the ship was British, not American, even though 128 of the 1,198 killed were Americans; second, the Germans warned in advance that they would torpedo ships on the open seas; third, the *Lusitania* was carrying small arms ammunition [so it wasn't a neutral ship]; and finally, the ship was sunk on May 7, 1915, and the Americans didn't declare war on Germany until April 6, 1917 [nearly two years later].

RUN AWAY!

On June 4, 1754, a twenty-one-year-old lieutenant colonel in the Virginia militia and his men were ordered to build a fort and confront the French forces near what is now Pittsburgh. When they got to the location, they discovered the French had already occupied a fort called Duquesne. So the young officer attacked a French work party, took some prisoners, and then hurriedly constructed the aptly named Fort Necessity. The French immediately attacked, surrounded the newly constructed fort, and sent the lieutenant colonel and his men back to Virginia where, oddly enough, he was hailed as a hero. Unwittingly, the young Lieutenant Colonel George Washington had ordered the shots that began the French and Indian War.

WHAT'S YOUR SIGN?

Benjamin Franklin was the only person to put his signature on all four primary documents that created the United States of America: the Treaty of Peace with Great Britain, the Declaration of Independence, the Treaty of Alliance with France, and the Constitution of the United States.

RUN, JESSE, RUN

After Jesse Owens won a gold medal in the 1936 Olympics in Berlin, Germany, Adolf Hitler refused to shake his hand because he was black. This would certainly fit the impression we have of Hitler, but the story just isn't true. It's true that Hitler didn't congratulate Owens, but he didn't congratulate any of the winners, even citizens of his own country, after the first day of the Olympics. That's because he was abiding by the International Olympic Committee's recommendation that he remain neutral. Owens even stood up for Hitler when he said, "Hitler didn't snub me——it was FDR who snubbed me. The president didn't even send me a telegram." Owens recalled that he had received the greatest ovations of his career in the Olympic Stadium in Berlin.

NOT LIKE THE WEST

The popular image of the early history of the Old West as a rough-and-tumble, shoot 'em up, violent, gun-fighting, homicidal era in American history is highly overrated——or, in other words, not really true. The main perpetrators of this image are the pulp fiction writers and, of course, Hollywood. In fact, more people die in most individual Hollywood westerns than died in an entire year in the West's toughest towns. In 1878, the most violent year in Dodge City, only five people were killed. In the South Dakota town of Deadwood, only four people were killed in its most homicidal year. And in Tombstone, Arizona, the infamous hometown of the shoot-out at the OK Corral in 1881, only five people were killed [three during the shoot-out].

NOT ALL BLACK AND WHITE

If a question on a history test asked whether it was the North or the South that first forbade slavery, most people would answer the North. Surprisingly, that event first took place in the South——the deep South, in fact——in Georgia. In 1735, three years after Georgia was founded, its trustees outlawed the importation of blacks to the colony to forestall slavery. A short fifteen years later, under tremendous pressure from big planters, the trustees reversed their decision and allowed blacks to be brought into the colony as slaves.

GERALD FORD WAS SWORN IN AS PRESIDENT A SHORT
TWENTY-EIGHT MINUTES AFTER THE SECRETARY OF STATE
RECEIVED RICHARD NIXON'S LETTER OF RESIGNATION.

A WING AND A PRAYER

Here's another George Washington myth that has burrowed its way into our national consciousness: the image of General Washington kneeling in the snow at Valley Forge deep in prayer. The story came from Mason Locke Weems [generally referred to as Parson Weems], the same man who created the "Washington chopped down the cherry tree" myth. In 1918, the Valley Forge Park Commission issued a report stating, "In none of these [documents] were found a single paragraph that will substantiate the tradition of the 'Prayer at Valley Forge.'" But still the image lives on.

PHOTOS DON'T LIE

Another endearing American image [and one used in dozens of history books] is Thomas Hill's rendition of the golden spike ceremony. The ceremony was in celebration of the First Transcontinental Railroad, connecting the Union Pacific and Central Pacific railroads, on May 10, 1869, at Promontory Summit, Utah. Hill's painting shows women in formal, elegant dresses, and men in fancy frock coats standing in front of several beautiful fluttering American flags. The actual photograph of the event shows something entirely different: Most of the men were wearing work clothes, several holding liquor bottles and looking intoxicated, and there were also a few sleazy-looking camp prostitutes.

NO PLACE LIKE HOME

The myths surrounding the Pilgrims are so numerous that one even involves what type of housing they lived in. Many Americans believe, usually because of artists' paintings, that the Pilgrims lived in log cabins. They didn't. The Pilgrims were English so they brought with them traditional English building construction methods, and that certainly wouldn't have been log cabins. The Germans and the Swedes introduced log cabins nearly a century later, and there's no record of the term "log cabin" being used before the 1770s. Although we have no definitive proof of what a Pilgrim house looked like, it would probably have been a simple frame structure [due to the plentiful amount of wood]. We do know that by late 1621 they had constructed seven dwellings for communal living, including four storehouses, and two years later they had twenty houses standing.

THE REAL CASEY JONES

Casey Jones is the legendary railroad folk hero——the man who sacrificed his life to save the lives of the passengers on his train. He *is* legendary, and he *is* a hero——because he was a real person and not a myth. John Luther "Casey" Jones [1863—1900] was an American railroad engineer from Jackson, Tennessee, who worked for the Illinois Central Railroad. On April 30, 1900, his fireman Sim Webb was shoveling coal when he saw the signal flags and red lights of a stopped freight train on the same track ahead of them. Jones told Webb to jump, which he did, and by staying at the controls and bringing the speed of his train down from seventy-five to thirty-five miles an hour, he saved the lives of the passengers on his train. Jones was the only person to die in the wreck, and he was immortalized for his courage in a popular ballad sung by his friend Wallace Saunders.

DON'T HAVE A COW, MAN II

Many of us are familiar with the story of Mrs. O'Leary's cow kicking over a lantern and starting the Great Chicago Fire of 1871, and much of it is true. The fire did start in Catherine O'Leary's barn house at 137 DeKoven Street, and she did have a cow. But whether the cow was the true culprit is the center of the controversial myth. The fire probably started while her son James and two of his friends, Daniel "Pegleg" Sullivan and Louis M. Cohn, were gambling in the barn. When Mrs. O'Leary came out around 9 p.m. to chase them away, the lantern got knocked over by mistake. Michael Ahern, a *Chicago Tribune* reporter, admitted several years after the fire that he had made up the story of the cow kicking over the lantern because it was more interesting copy.

THE SITE OF MRS. O'LEARY'S BARN NOW HOUSES
THE CHICAGO FIRE DEPARTMENT TRAINING SCHOOL.

PUMPING IRONY

It may sound like a tragically ironic myth that on the night the *Titanic* sank they were showing the film *The Poseidon Adventure,* about a group of people trying to stay alive after their ocean liner capsized. But it's true. Two films were scheduled during the voyage and both had nautical themes: The 1911 movie *The Lighthouse Keeper* starring Mary Pickford played on the evenings of April 12 and 13, and *The Poseidon Adventure,* directed by D. W. Griffith, played on April 14. The movie began at 11 p.m. and people were so enthralled by the action, they didn't notice their ship jolting when it hit the fatal iceberg forty minutes later.

ONE HUMP OR TWO?

In 1856, Secretary of War Jefferson Davis [who several years later would become the president of the Confederate States of America] ordered seventy camels brought to the United States from the Middle East. Davis realized that camels would be much better suited for travels across desert regions, didn't need much water, could eat desert vegetation, and could carry more than even the largest horse or mule could carry. The U.S. Camel Corps was established at Camp Verde, Texas, in the hill country north of San Antonio. But the camels didn't work out as expected; they were very stubborn, required special handlers, and scared the horses. In less than two years, the entire Corps was dismantled and a number of the camels were set loose in the desert.

In the mid-1870s, one of the abandoned camels wandered into Fort Selden, New Mexico, territory. The strange beast terrified the post commander's young son, who ran to hide behind his mother. The commander was Captain Arthur MacArthur, whose son grew up to be General of the Army Douglas MacArthur.

DON'T EARN AN "A"

The Puritans in Salem, Massachusetts, passed a law in 1695 that imposed severe punishment on a person convicted of the crime of adultery. First, the perpetrator would have to wear the letter "A" on a conspicuous part of his or her clothes for the rest of their lives [which inspired Nathaniel Hawthorne's story *The Scarlet Letter*].

An adulterer could also receive forty lashes from a whip and be required to sit on the gallows, with chains around the neck, for at least one hour. However, in the seventeenth century the penalty for adultery in Massachusetts was death. Even with this form of punishment looming over their heads, when the population of Boston hovered around 4,000 people, there were still forty-eight children born out of wedlock and fifty instances of fornication.

TWO-TIMING,
TWO-YEAR PRESIDENT

During his short two-year term, the twenty-ninth president of the United States, Warren Harding, was known for only a few things: having a corrupt administration, gambling, and womanizing. Before he became president, he had an affair with a woman named Carrie Phillips who demanded marriage although she was still married to someone else at the time. She had all of Harding's love letters and threatened to blackmail him even though he had already given her a Cadillac and promised her $5,000 a year. His campaign manager, Albert Lasker, bought her vow of silence with an all-expense-paid trip around the world [with her husband] under the condition that they depart before the election and not return until after.

Harding also had an affair with a woman named Nan Britton, with whom he was cheating on both his wife, Florence, and his mistress, Carrie Phillips. Britton was a virgin when they first met, and they continued their relationship while Harding was in office. It was known that when Nan visited the White House, they would sneak off and have sex in a small five-by-five-foot coat closet.

I'LL GRANT YOU THAT

There have been a few notorious presidential siblings, such as Billy Carter, Roger Clinton, Sam Houston Johnson, and "Big Don" Nixon, but none of them hold a candle to the likes of Ulysses S. Grant's younger brother, Orvil. Orvil and Grant's secretary of war, William Belknap, hit upon the idea of demanding kickbacks from the franchising of highly profitable trading posts on the western front. Because of regulations, soldiers were forced to exclusively use army trading posts to make purchases. The money demanded by Grant and Belknap forced the trading post owners to jack up their prices so high that General George Armstrong Custer complained. Custer even testified against Belknap and implicated Orvil Grant during a Senate investigation——another reason why the administration of Ulysses S. Grant is considered the most scandal-ridden of all presidencies.

GO WITH THE FLOW

Would you believe that an earthquake once reversed the course of the Mississippi River? The truth is, it wasn't one earthquake but three in 1811 and 1812 that changed the river's course. The New Madrid Fault Zone, which lies between Memphis and St. Louis, experienced three earthquakes registering approximately 8 on the Richter scale. They sent shockwaves along the Mississippi and altered the river's flow.

FRANKLIN D. ROOSEVELT SERVED A RECORD 4,422 DAYS AS PRESIDENT OF THE UNITED STATES.

NEARLY A DUAL DUEL

On July 11, 1804, Vice President Aaron Burr killed Alexander Hamilton during a duel. In 1797, Hamilton had nearly dueled with future president James Monroe, and it was Aaron Burr who stepped in and stopped the confrontation. After his duel with Hamilton, Burr was charged with murder in both New York and New Jersey, but neither case ever went to trial. To let the smoke settle, Burr fled to South Carolina but soon returned to Washington, D.C., and finished out his term as vice president.

SHUT YOUR MOUTH!

For reasons still unknown, Texas Congressman Thomas Lindsay Blanton, a Presbyterian Sunday-school teacher and prohibitionist, inserted dirty words into the *Congressional Record* in 1921. His colleagues overwhelmingly censured him on October 24, 1921, by a vote of 293—0.

THE FIRST MOTTO THAT APPEARED ON U.S. COINS WAS NOT
"IN GOD WE TRUST"; IT WAS "MIND YOUR BUSINESS."
THESE COPPER CENTS WERE AUTHORIZED ON APRIL 21, 1787.

A REAL SIX-SHOOTER

Political duels usually leave one person dead or wounded, but rarely do they cause laughter. One exception was the case of the 1836 duel between two congressmen, Jesse Bynum of North Carolina and Daniel Jenifer of Maryland. Bynum loudly objected to Jenifer's denouncement of the course of President Jackson's party, and after a brief shouting match they were off to a shooting match. Both men arrived at the Bladensburg Dueling Ground, paced off ten feet, and fired. No one was hit. So they reloaded and shot again. Again, they both missed. The same result happened on the third, fourth, and fifth shots. As they prepared for the sixth round, Bynum's pistol accidentally discharged. One of Jenifer's seconds leveled his pistol at Bynum, but Jenifer ordered him to halt. Then Jenifer aimed carefully at Bynum, pulled the trigger——and missed. The duel was called off, and the two dishonored men agreed to a draw.

HE WAS PASTY WHITE

It was one of the most reported political sex scandals of the
1970s——the story of Arkansas Representative Wilbur Mills
and notorious stripper Fanne Foxe. U.S. Park Police stopped Mills,
chairman of the powerful House Ways and Means Committee, in the
early morning hours of October 7, 1974, for speeding with his lights
off. Mills had four companions in the car and one of them, Fanne
Foxe, stepped out and jumped into the murky waters of Washington's
Tidal Basin. Mills, who was intoxicated, had a bloody nose and several
scratches on his face that he claimed were the result of trying to restrain
Foxe. But a little scandal between the most powerful man in Congress
and a stripper wasn't enough to bother the good people of Arkansas, who
re-elected Mills to another term.

THE REAL FALL GUY

It's an event in American history that is frequently referenced when discussions of political corruption surface: the Teapot Dome Scandal. But what exactly was it, and what's with the weird name? In 1922, the U.S. secretary of the interior under Warren Harding, Albert B. Fall, leased the Teapot Dome oil reserves [so named because of the site's resemblance to a giant sandstone teapot] without competitive bidding. He also leased other oil fields in exchange for "loans" amounting to $400,000 from Harry Sinclair and E. L. Doheny, multimillionaire oil producers doing business as Mammoth Oil Company and Pan-American Petroleum and Transport Company, respectively. What makes the scandal historical, apart from its catchy name, is that Fall became the first cabinet member in history to serve time in prison.

SAY IT AIN'T SO, JOE

Wisconsin Senator Joe McCarthy, notorious for the communist witch-hunts of the 1950s, was first elected after campaigning on a much-touted record of military service during World War II, christening himself "Tail-Gunner Joe." But McCarthy never actually served as a tail-gunner——he flew as a gunner-observer. He later claimed to have flown thirty-two missions when, in fact, he had only flown twelve.

SICKLES IN A PICKLE

Congressman Dan Sickles is known for a number of things: as a Union general in the Civil War, as a U.S. minister to Spain, for being censured by the New York State Assembly for escorting known prostitute Fanny White into its chambers, and for being the first man in U.S. history to use temporary insanity as a legal defense. In 1859, Sickles was accused of murdering his wife's paramour, Philip Barton Key, son of Francis Scott Key. And although he confessed to the murder, his lawyer claimed he had been driven temporarily insane by his wife's infidelity. The public loved him [because he was protecting other innocent women from the evil lustfulness of Key], and apparently, the jury bought it: Sickles was acquitted.

Sickles went on to win the Congressional Medal of Honor for his acts of bravery during the Civil War and for the fact that he got one of his legs blown off during the Battle of Gettysburg.

THE BUNNY HOP

Collectors love to acquire the first edition of their favorite magazines. But if you're looking for the first issue of *Playboy* dated December 1, 1953——you're out of luck. There is no such issue. When Hugh Hefner published the first issue of *Playboy* he didn't know if there would be a second and, therefore, decided not to date it. Interestingly enough, *Playboy* was first titled *Stag Party*, but the publisher of a hunting magazine called *Stag* forced Hefner to rename his girly magazine.

The story that Hugh Hefner took the nude photograph of his first centerfold, Marilyn Monroe, on rumpled red velvet, is an urban legend. Photographer Tom Kelly made the now infamous photograph in 1949, and it had already appeared in calendars before Hefner paid $500 for the rights to use it in his magazine.

A MICKEY MOUSE OPERATION

One of the most underreported protests of the early 1970s was the Yippies' invasion of Disneyland on August 6, 1970. Hundreds of long-haired youths reacted to leaflets and advertisements placed in the *Los Angeles Free Press* inviting "Yippies" to attend the First International "Yippie Pow Wow" at Disneyland——lovingly called "Yippie Day." The Yippies were encouraged to attend this non-sponsored event "to liberate Minnie Mouse, have free rein of the park and infiltrate Tom Sawyer's Island." The other causes listed were for a Women's Lib rally to free Tinkerbell and a Black Panther hot breakfast at Aunt Jemima's. Disneyland decided to close early even though there was no violence, and most of the Yippies simply acted Goofy.

I OBJECT!

Highly acclaimed marksman and World War I hero Alvin Cullum York [1887—1964] from Pall Mall, Tennessee, earned the Medal of Honor for capturing, along with seven other men, 132 Germans during the Meuse-Argonne Offensive in France. "Sergeant York," as he will forever be known, although he was only a corporal at the time, did capture a German machine gun nest on October 8, 1918, killing twenty-eight Germans, capturing thirty-two machine guns, and taking 132 Germans prisoner. But before he became a hero, York, a deeply religious man, had applied to be a conscientious objector to the war. However, because his religion [Church of Christ in Christian Union] wasn't recognized as a church at the time, he was drafted into the Army.

Oh, Say Can You See?

We've all heard the story of how Francis Scott Key, watching the bombardment of Fort McHenry during the Battle of Baltimore on the night of September 13, 1814, was so awestruck that he wrote a little poem that turned into the national anthem of the United States, *The Star Spangled Banner*. Key was approximately eight miles away during the attack and couldn't have possibly seen the normal "storm flag," a small flag designed expressly for bad weather, which flew during the battle and the night. According to the eyewitness testimony of Midshipman Robert J. Barrettas, as the British fleet sailed away the next morning, the Americans "hoisted a most superb and splendid ensign on their battery." This flag, which is on display at the Smithsonian in Washington, D.C., is enormous: thirty feet by forty-two feet. So what Keys saw "so gallantly streaming" was the newly hoisted flag——not the flag that flew during the battle.

DUMB ASS

How did the Democrats become known as the party of the donkey? It all started when Andrew Jackson ran for president in 1828 with the slogan, "Let the people rule," and his opponents tried to label him a "jackass." Jackson, however, turned the tables on his "neigh"-sayers by using the donkey, representing his stubbornness, on his campaign posters.

The Donkey symbol of the Democrat party was first used in a political cartoon in 1837 titled "A Modern Baalim and his Ass." Again the symbol was used in conjunction with Andrew Jackson. Even though he had left office by this time, he still thought of himself as the party's leader. He was shown in the cartoon trying to push the donkey where he wanted it to go.

CHILD'S PLAY

Samuel Slater [1768—1835] was popularly known as the "Founder of the American Industrial Revolution," but he was also the founder of something else——the use of child labor. Slater's mill opened in Pawtucket, Rhode Island, in 1793 and started with nine workers, all of them children under the age of twelve. By 1830, 55 percent of the mill workers in Rhode Island were children.

DURING THE CIVIL WAR AND ESPECIALLY IN MILITARY PRISONS, ILLNESS AND DISEASE WERE SO COMMON THAT TWICE AS MANY SOLDIERS DIED OF SICKNESS AS DIED IN BATTLE.

SUPPLY AND DEMAND

The term GI is used to describe members of the United States armed forces or equipment issued by the U.S. government. It is widely believed that the term GI therefore stands for "Government Issue" or "General Issue" or even "General Infantry." But on supply records, the initials originally preceded any equipment made from galvanized iron, such as trashcans. American soldiers during World War I commonly referred to incoming German artillery shells as "GI cans." The term slowly morphed, and by World War II it meant anything issued by the government——including soldiers.

AFTER LEAVING OFFICE, PRESIDENT CALVIN "SILENT CAL"
COOLIDGE WENT ON TO WRITE A NATIONALLY SYNDICATED
NEWSPAPER COLUMN, "CALVIN COOLIDGE SAYS,"
FROM 1930 TO 1931.

THE EAGLE HAS LANDED

I t has been rumored that the Seal of the President of the United States, which shows an eagle holding an olive branch in its left talon and arrows in the other, is modified so that the eagle's head is turned to signify whether we're at war or peace. But it's not true. According to Bill Allman, White House curator, there is just one Seal of the President and the head faces toward the olive branch. This rumor might have started because before 1945, the eagle's head did face the arrows. President Harry Truman had it modified after World War II.

By Any Means Necessary

President Lyndon Johnson needed a reason to launch a full-scale invasion of Vietnam but couldn't justify it to the American people——until three North Vietnamese patrol ships fired on an American ship keeping watch on the Tonkin Gulf. Two days later, there was a report that a second attack on American ships was under way, and the president pleaded with Congress for action. This second attack provoked Congress to pass the Gulf of Tonkin Resolution on August 10, 1964, giving Johnson authorization, without a formal declaration of war by Congress, to use military force in Southeast Asia. But the second attack never happened, and it was known that it hadn't happened by Johnson's administration. But it's what they needed to ramp up what would become known as the Vietnam War.

The Gulf of Tonkin Resolution unanimously passed the House with only forty minutes of debate. Congress wasn't aware that the resolution had been drafted several months before the Gulf of Tonkin Incident ever took place.

A WAKE-UP CALL

During the days of the Pilgrims, church services weren't confined to today's standard one-hour sermon. In fact, they would routinely go on for up to seven hours. So how did the Pilgrims keep people awake that long? A simple device, which consisted of a wooden ball on the end of a length of string, served to bonk the nodding member of the congregation awake.

IRONICALLY, THE CONSTITUTION OF THE CONFEDERATE STATES OF AMERICA FORBADE THE PRACTICE OF IMPORTING SLAVES FROM OUTSIDE THE CONFEDERACY.

LOOK IT UP

Infamous American dictionary maker Noah Webster adamantly hated the British and was simultaneously filled with American pride. He thought total separation from the English and their language was in order. "America must be as independent in literature as she is in politics," he wrote, and for him that included freedom from British spelling. Webster published his first dictionary, *A Compendious Dictionary of the English Language*, in 1806, and included his Americanized spellings. "Centre" was changed to "center," "honour" to "honor," and "programme" to "program." "Colour" became "color," "theatre" changed to "theater," "travelling" to "traveling," and so on. But his attempt to change "tongue" to "tung" didn't meet with much success.

SPARE THE ROD

Connecticut laws in the late 1600s were, to say the least, strict. Here is one example:

> "If any man have a stubborn or rebellious Son, of sufficient understanding and years, viz. fifteen years of age, which will not obey the voice of his Father, or the voice of his Mother, and that when they have chastened him, he will not hearken unto them; then may his Father or Mother, being his natural Parents, lay hold on him, and bring him to the Magistrates assembled in Court, and testified unto them, that their Son is Stubborn and Rebellious, and will not obey their voice and chastisement, but lives in sundry notorious Crimes, such a Son shall be put to death, Deut. 21: 20. 21."

The Deut. 21:20.21 reference denotes that the city elders got this law from that particular passage from Deuteronomy in the Bible.

DOUBTING THOMAS

In 1801, Vice President Thomas Jefferson presented to Congress his *Manual of Parliamentary Practice*, in part because of the occasional tantrums that erupted in the Senate. One telling passage reads as if it had been written by a teacher of an unruly classroom: "No one is to disturb another in his speech by hissing, coughing, spitting, speaking or whispering to another; nor to stand up or interrupt him; nor to pass between the Speaker and the speaking member; nor to go across the [Senate chamber], or to walk up and down it, or to take books or papers from the [clerk's] table, or write there."

STUPID AMERICAN HISTORY

STILL SEEMS LIKE A GOOD IDEA

On April 27, 1911, Congressman Victor Berger of Wisconsin introduced a constitutional amendment to the House of Representatives that would abolish . . . the Senate. The preamble to the amendment read, "Whereas the Senate in particular has become an obstructive and useless body, a menace to the liberties of the people, and an obstacle to social growth." A Congressional committee quickly and quietly squashed the amendment.

NOT WITH A BANG

The Civil War got its start during the Battle of Fort Sumter in Charleston Harbor, South Carolina, on April 12, 1861. One would think that a battle that kicked off such a war would have been bloody with a high body count, but it wasn't. In fact, no one died during the one-day battle. There was a casualty, however, when Private Daniel Hough was killed when the cannon he was loading accidentally discharged. That incident happened on April 14, the day after the battle ended, during a surrender ceremony.

THE CHOSEN PEOPLE

It was called General Order No. 11, and it was the instructions for the expulsion of all Jews in particular military districts during a war——but it wasn't World War II and the person who issued the order wasn't Hitler. It was Major General Ulysses S. Grant and the order was issued on December 17, 1862, during the American Civil War. Grant was convinced that "mostly Jews and other unprincipled traders" were controlling the black-market trade in Southern cotton in Tennessee, Mississippi, and Kentucky. President Abraham Lincoln revoked the order a few weeks later following an outcry of protest from Jewish community leaders and members of both the press and Congress. Grant later shifted the blame to a subordinate, claiming he had written the order and Grant had just added his signature without reading the document.

STONE COLD STONEWALL

During the Battle of Chancellorsville, Virginia, from April 30 to May 6, 1863, Confederate General Thomas "Stonewall" Jackson gave strict orders to shoot any unknown or unidentified solider who approached their lines and to ask questions later. And, you guessed it, when Jackson and some of his men were returning from a reconnaissance mission, they were fired upon by their own troops. Jackson was wounded in his left arm; eight days later it was amputated. Following complications from pneumonia, Jackson died. He was considered by many to be the best strategist in the Confederate Army and quite possibly of either side.

YOU CAN RING MY BELL

The story of the Liberty Bell as we know it today came from an 1847 book entitled *Washington and His Generals: or, Legends of the American Revolution* by George Lippard, a Philadelphia journalist. Lippard was the one who created the whole story of the bell's involvement in American independence, and thus he forged forever one of the greatest mythical symbols of American freedom.

**PRESIDENT LINCOLN HAD FOUR BROTHERS-IN-LAW
WHO FOUGHT FOR THE CONFEDERACY.**

ICE CAPADES

The theory has been that the *Titanic* sank because of a 300-foot gash that cut through the hull and all the watertight holds, dooming the ship to sink. But a naval architect who was on an expedition to uncover some of the mysteries of the *Titanic* has proven that the damage wasn't nearly as extensive as previously believed. In fact, the whole area of impact added up to only about twelve square feet. But it was the location of the damage that sank the unsinkable ship. It was a series of six thin openings across the *Titanic*'s starboard hull, directly over six critical watertight holds.

I'M OK, YOU'RE OK

Technically, there never was a shoot-out at the O.K. Corral. You see, the shoot-out actually took place in a vacant lot between Harwood's house and Fly's Lodging House, nearly a quarter of a block away from the O.K. Corral. But it was referred to as the "Shoot-Out at the O.K. Corral" because "Shoot-Out by Fly's Lodging House" wasn't a suitable alternative.

MARK MY WORD

The second half of *The Adventures of Huckleberry Finn* has been in the Erie County Public Library since the late 1800s, but no one knew what happened to the first half. That is, until 1990 when the first several chapters of the book were literally found in an old trunk in an attic. This trunk belonged to the late James Fraser Gluck, who was a benefactor of the library while he was alive. Evidently, Gluck convinced Twain to send the manuscript to him for the library, decided to take it home to read, and then forgot about it. Gluck died unexpectedly at the age of forty-five in 1897, ten years after the manuscript had been presented to the library. It is assumed that since there was no title page to denote what it was, the manuscript was simply put into a trunk when Gluck's estate was settled.

THE SHORTEST WAR IN AMERICAN HISTORY WAS THE
SPANISH–AMERICAN WAR. IT LASTED FIVE MONTHS,
FROM APRIL 25 TO AUGUST 12, 1898.

A Captive Audience

The Alien and Sedition Acts stifled not only newspaper reporters and editors but also some members of Congress. Representative Matthew Lyon of Vermont was sent to jail for four months and fined $1,000 for criticizing President John Adams in a Vermont newspaper. However, his constituents came to his aid, took up a collection to pay his fine, and made him the first congressman to be elected, or reelected in his case, to office while still in jail.

One of the original four parts of the Alien and Sedition Acts enacted on July 6, 1798, The Alien Enemies Act [officially "An Act Respecting Alien Enemies"], authorized the president to apprehend and deport resident aliens if their home countries were at war with the United States. That act was signed into law with no expiration date and it remains in effect today as 50 U.S.C. § 21-24.

IT WAS THE FIRST SECOND-RATE BURGLARY

It was a second-rate burglary of a Democrat party office, but it wasn't in Washington, D.C., and it had nothing to do with President Richard Nixon. This break-in took place in 1930 and was ordered by President Herbert Hoover. According to the diary of Glenn Howell, a naval intelligence officer, he and Robert J. Peterkin were ordered by Hoover after "he received a confidential report alleging that the Democrats had accumulated a file of data so damaging that if made public it would destroy both his reputation and his entire Administration." Howell wrote that they had searched the office but found nothing of consequence.

KEEP IT IN THE FAMILY

We would like to believe that the United States does not now have, nor ever has had, a royal family or a monarchial system of government. But if you look at the bloodline of certain presidents, you'll see that a number of them have something in common——each other. Take, for example, the thirty-second president of the United States, Franklin Delano Roosevelt [1882—1945]. He was a relative of William Howard Taft, Theodore Roosevelt, Benjamin Harrison, Ulysses S. Grant, Zachary Taylor, William Henry Harrison, Martin Van Buren, John Quincy Adams, James Madison, John Adams, and George Washington.

ARREST MAYOR MCCHEESE

I guess you could call this a second-rate hamburglary. Richard Nixon, infamous for the second-rate burglary known as the Watergate scandal, was also accused of illegally raising the price of the McDonald's Quarter Pounder from 59 cents to 65 cents. Included in the Articles of Impeachment against Richard Nixon was "21. Bribery, Fraud. Solicited and obtained for the reelection campaign of President Nixon, in June, July and August, 1972, from Ray A. Kroc, Chairman of the Board of McDonald's, Inc., contributions of $200,000, in exchange for permission from the Price Commission, first denied on May 21, 1972, then granted on September 8, 1972, to raise the price of the McDonald's quarterpounder cheeseburger, in violation of article II, section 4 of the Constitution and Section 201, 372, 872 and 1505 of the Criminal Code."

A Real Land Ho

As his crews were on the verge of mutiny, Columbus heard the words he had been praying for——land had been sighted. On October 12, 1492, a lookout named Rodrigo de Triana aboard the *Pinta* saw moonlight reflecting off a distant shore. The lookout was extremely excited, not just for his discovery, but also because he knew Columbus had promised a substantial reward to the first person who sighted land. But Columbus claimed he had seen the reflection the night before and didn't want to excite the crew. So he kept the reward for himself.

Thomas Jefferson wrote the Declaration of Independence in just eighteen days.

GOING FOR THE GOLD

Another American propagandist belief about the 1936 Olympics is that Hitler was outraged because a few black athletes walked away with the majority of medals and left the Aryans hanging their blond heads in shame. A quick, simple look at the record proves this is a false belief. Hitler was quite pleased with his country's endeavors in the games because Germany was awarded the most medals. The Germans won thirty-three Gold, twenty-six Silver, and thirty Bronze for a total of eighty-nine medals. The next biggest winner was the United States with a total of fifty-six medals.

IN NAME ONLY

The Hudson River, the Hudson Strait, and Hudson Bay are all named after one man, the navigator and sea explorer Henry Hudson. In 1610, Hudson was financed by a group of English merchants to find the Northwest Passage, connecting the Atlantic to the Pacific Ocean, and thus Europe with the Orient. Hudson thought he was on the right track, but he headed south into what is now James Bay, and his ships became stuck in the ice. After a brutal winter in 1611, his crew was frustrated with Hudson, and they abandoned him, his son, and eleven crew members in a small boat and set them adrift. Hudson was never heard from again. It was not until the 1850s that Sir Robert McClure discovered a route through the Canadian Arctic.

GIVEN THE BOOT

The Boot Monument located in Saratoga National Historical Park in New York was erected in honor of Benedict Arnold's heroism, his victory in the Battles of Saratoga, and for the injury he sustained to his leg during the battle. The monument is dedicated to "the most brilliant soldier of the Continental army . . . winning for his countrymen the decisive battle of the American Revolution and for himself the rank of Major General." But because he later became a turncoat, the monument does not mention his name and is distinguished as the only war memorial in the United States that does not say whom it commemorates.

GEORGIA ON MY MIND

James Oglethorpe originally founded the colony of Georgia in 1732. He was granted a Royal Charter because of his intention to recruit settlers from English debtors prisons, which would theoretically rid England of its so-called undesirable elements. Oglethorpe also outlawed slavery. Another reason for Georgia's significance was that it was a buffer between South Carolina and possible attacks from Spanish Florida and French Louisiana.

DON'T LOSE YOUR HEAD

Savage Indians going on scalping raids is an enduring image in the mythic world of the Old West. But it wasn't the American Indian who first started the scalping tradition——it was the Dutch. During the early 1700s, the Dutch initiated the "scalp bounty": A fee was paid for Indian scalps. And in 1763, Benjamin Franklin pushed the Pennsylvania legislature to approve a bounty on Indian scalps as a way of placating a group of angry frontiersmen [the Paxton Boys] who complained the government wasn't doing enough to protect them.

OH, BROTHER!

Randolph Jefferson is a name that most people don't know. But if I mention his more memorable brother Thomas, then everyone knows who he was. Like most people who are compared to Thomas Jefferson, Randolph comes up short in the brains department. But it's possible that Randolph might actually have been somewhat dimwitted. Even one self-effacing Monticello slave named Isaac said this about him: "He was one mighty simple man——used to come out among the black people, play the fiddle and dance half the night; hadn't much more sense than Isaac."

A SYMBOLIC GESTURE

Shortly after the Boston Massacre, which of course was named by the Patriots as a propaganda move, Henry Pelham made an engraving of the shootings. Paul Revere "borrowed" the engraving and did one of his own——surprisingly enough, Revere's engraving got to the printers first and is now considered a patriotic icon.

LA LA LAND

Spanish governor Felipe de Neve founded what is now the city of Los Angeles on September 4, 1781, and named it *El Pueblo de Nuestra Señora la Reina de los Ángeles de la Porciúncula* [The Village of Our Lady, the Queen of the Angels of the Little Portion]. That's why L.A. is called "The City of Angels."

Born in Vienna, Associate Justice Felix Frankfurter is the only naturalized American ever to serve on the Supreme Court. He was appointed to the Court in 1939 and served until his voluntary retirement in 1962.

LOVE A MAN IN UNIFORM

The Battles of Lexington and Concord spilled the first blood of the American Revolutionary War on April 19, 1775. So when the Second Continental Congress met in Philadelphia on May 10, 1775, they realized that if they acted quickly, they would have the opportunity to bottle up the whole of the British army in Boston. One of the most underrated founding fathers, John Adams, knew that to solidify the ranks of Congress, they would have to win over the delegates of the South. And the solution was already in the room: George Washington, decked out in his old military uniform that he hadn't worn since 1758, was officially given the appointment of commander-in-chief of the Continental Army on June 15, 1775.

OH, HALE!

On the short list of well-known American patriotic heroes is Nathan Hale, primarily remembered for his famous last words, "I only regret that I have but one life to lose for my country"——which, of course, he probably never said. Frederick MacKensie, a British officer and eyewitness at the time of Hale's death, wrote in his diary that Hale said he "thought it the duty of every good Officer, to obey any orders given him by his Commander-in-Chief." Not as memorable, perhaps, but probably closer to the truth. But who was Nathan Hale? He is considered America's first spy, and on his very first mission, he was captured in possession of maps showing British troop positions. After he confessed, Hale was hanged on September 22, 1776.

ELEVATING OTIS

James Otis [1725—1783] could be considered the lost founding father. He was a Boston lawyer and the man who came up with the battle cry of the American Revolution, "Taxation without representation is Tyranny." It was Otis who first fought against British authority by defending a group of sixty-three Boston merchants against the "writs of assistance," basically Parliament's legal way of sanctioning unwarranted search and seizure. But the reason Otis is swept under the historical carpet is that he went a little wacky [some historians believe he suffered from bipolar disorder or schizophrenia] and became an embarrassment. Otis didn't die on July 4 as did two of the other founding fathers. He went out with more of a bang, having been struck by lightning in May 1783.

WARREN G. HARDING AND JOHN F. KENNEDY WERE THE ONLY PRESIDENTS TO HAVE BEEN SURVIVED BY THEIR FATHERS.

THE LIZARD KING

During James Madison's second presidential term in 1812, two new political traditions were created. First, no sitting president has lost a reelection campaign during a time of war; and second, Madison's vice president, Elbridge Gerry, a signer of the Declaration of Independence, was the first politician to redistrict, or carve up, a state to give his party an advantage during the next election. His opponents complained the districts weren't symmetrical and had the shapes of slithering salamanders. A new word entered the political lexicon: "gerrymander."

THE REAL SPIRIT OF ST. LOUIS

In the early 1940s, he warned Jews in America to "shut up" and accused "Jewish-owned media" of trying to push the United States into World War II. Sounds like Adolf Hitler, but it was actually the beloved national hero Charles Lindbergh. Lindbergh, along with Henry Ford, was very conservative. Both were isolationists and held strong anti-Semitic political views. Lindberg visited Germany on several occasions to inspect the Luftwaffe [German air force] and, in 1938, was presented with a medal by Hermann Göring, founder of the Gestapo and Hitler's air minister. Not to be outdone, Henry Ford received a medal from Hitler himself in 1938.

A ROSE BY ANY OTHER NAME

When one thinks of the most notorious traitors in American history two names leap to mind: Benedict Arnold and Tokyo Rose. But there's one major difference between these two——Tokyo Rose never existed. The woman whom most would associate with the personification of Tokyo Rose would be Iva Toguri D'Aquino, who broadcast as "Orphan Ann" on Radio Tokyo [NHK]. Other women who might have claimed the moniker were Ruth Hayakawa [who substituted for D'Aquino on weekends], June Suyama ["The Nightingale of Nanking"], or Myrtle Lipton ["Little Margie"].

A report from the U.S. Office of War Information published in the *New York Times* in August 1945 announced "There is no Tokyo Rose; the name is strictly a GI invention.... Government monitors listening in twenty-four hours a day have never heard the word 'Tokyo Rose.'"

JACK OF ALL TRADES

George Washington was more than just the father of our country; he was the father of the first Mammoth Jackass. The existing jack donkeys during Washington's times were short in stature and didn't have the stamina Washington needed. So he imported donkeys from Spain and France. One donkey he received from the Marquis de Lafayette, named "Knight of Malta," was only about four-and-one-half feet tall, and Washington was very disappointed. So Washington bred Knight of Malta to his jennys and the outcome was the first American line of Mammoth Jacks——a breed name including both females and males.

JUST ADD SEX

Howard W. Smith, a Democratic congressman from Virginia, indicated his intention to keep the 1964 Civil Rights Act bottled up indefinitely and had what he thought was a foolproof plan. To the laughter of his House colleagues, Smith decided to add the word "sex" to the list of "race, color, religion, or national origin" that the bill had been designed to protect. Smith thought it would be the bill's death knell because he assumed nobody would vote to protect equality of the sexes, but he was wrong. The bill not only passed Congress, but it also passed the Senate and was then signed into law by President Lyndon Johnson on July 2, 1964.

WAIT A MINUTE, MAN

As Ralph Waldo Emerson put it in commemorating the Battle of Concord, "Here once the embattled farmers stood, And fired the shot heard round the world." Part of the romantic imagery of the American Revolution is that of the Minuteman. Ever ready, the Minuteman was a middle-class, dedicated sharpshooter who could be called out in a minute's time to come to the defense of the new nation. But these beliefs have little foundation in fact. Scholars have shown that most Minutemen came from the ranks of the poor and were paid for their services. They weren't sharpshooters; in fact, they weren't very good shots at all. But they could quickly assemble——mainly because they didn't have jobs and had nothing else to do.

WHAT ABOUT THE WHITES
OF THEIR EYES?

Captain John Parker, who commanded the Lexington militia at the Battle of Lexington on April 19, 1775, was quoted as saying, "Don't fire unless fired upon, but if they mean to have a war, let it begin here." It's doubtful he ever said it. The quote didn't surface until 1858 and was brought to everyone's attention by Parker's grandson, Theodore.

Civil War Union General Lew Wallace
[1827—1905] gained his greatest fame
not from activities on the battlefield
but as the author of the novel *Ben Hur:*
A Tale of the Christ.